T0164636

THE KNIGHT YEARS

Stories from a Young Pastor

Dr. Blair F. Rorabaugh

WestBow
PRESS
A DIVISION OF THOMAS NELSON

WestBow Press books may be ordered through booksellers or by contacting:

WestBow Press
A Division of Thomas Nelson
1663 Liberty Drive
Bloomington, IN 47403
www.westbowpress.com
1-(866) 928-1240

Because of the dynamic nature of the Internet, any web addresses or
links contained in this book may have changed since publication and
may no longer be valid. The views expressed in this work are solely those
of the author and do not necessarily reflect the views of the publisher,
and the publisher hereby disclaims any responsibility for them.

Any people depicted in stock imagery provided by Thinkstock are models,
and such images are being used for illustrative purposes only.
Certain stock imagery © Thinkstock.

Scripture taken from the Holy Bible, New International Version®.
Copyright © 1973, 1978, 1984 Biblica.
Used by permission of Zondervan. All rights reserved.

Scripture quotations marked "TLB" or "The Living Bible" are taken
from The Living Bible [computer file] / Kenneth N. Taylor. electronic
ed. Wheaton : Tyndale House, 1997, c1971 by Tyndale House
Publishers, Inc. Used by permission. All rights reserved.

ISBN: 978-1-4497-5974-2 (sc)
ISBN: 978-1-4497-5975-9 (e)

Library of Congress Control Number: 2012912759

Printed in the United States of America

WestBow Press rev. date: 7/19/2012

Dedicated to
Ben and Mary
Jerry, Lyndell and Dottie
the first to call me
Pastor

ACKNOWLEDGEMENTS

My life is the result of giving myself to God as a young child. My parents took me to church and we had family devotions in our home. It is not surprising that I desired to be a pastor. I thank God that He made it clear to me that this desire to be a minister of Jesus Christ was not my own but He put it in my heart. I would never have entered the ministry without the definite call of God in my life for along with the satisfaction there have been times of great distress.

The congregations I served have my gratitude and respect. Great churches build great pastors and my pastoral assignments have molded me as much as I have molded them. My people have been understanding and patient with me as I have learned to be the man of God in ministry. Thank you for every prayer and the many chicken dinners you invested in me as your pastor.

This book is the result of an illness that confined me to bed after the events of this book. I have forgotten the illness but not the thoughts that poured from me and I had to write them down. They lay dormant for many years waiting for the right time. God used even that time when I thought nothing was happening.

Cindy is my faithful companion in ministry who courageously has accepted my call as her call to serve and walk beside me in every church. Her gifts make her the model pastor's wife as well as my friend.

Thank you Nancy Tapsfield for editing my book, praying with me, and giving words of encouragement. Nancy, you are a gift to all who know you and God uses you.

The staff at WestBow are vigilant workers that have guided me through the process of producing a book. Thank you for nurturing this writer in what looked like an overwhelming task.

Contents

INTRODUCTION

A pastor's first church is like none other. His first assignment to minister as pastor only happens once, and each church is different. I count it a privilege to be a pastor, a minister of the Lord Jesus Christ. It is an honor to serve my Church. For each difficulty there have been many more blessings. For each discouragement there have been a hundred encouragers.

The stories I have written are true and as I remember. In every event there are as many stories as there are participants, and each person has a different view. These events are from my perspective.

In the early years of ministry, some of the things that happened to me and because of me, were the result of my philosophy of the knight on the royal charger, expediting the coming kingdom. Because I have aged or matured -- hopefully both -- I feel I can share them more objectively.

Where it has been necessary I have changed names to protect individuals or their families.

Faithful members, Ben and Mary Strode, still serve the church with distinction and humility. Ben read some of my material. When our memories are not always the same he is gracious and smiles at my memory of what happened. Some things a pastor is never allowed to disclose. I have honored that trust. Confidences that were shared with me are kept and most of them forgotten.

An advantage of the space of years is seeing how God works things out. In a recent visit to my first congregation and community I caught up with those I could locate. Many had gone to be with the Lord. They died triumphantly in the faith. Others are still faithful in one of several churches in the community. Some are not attending any church presently, but pastors always hope.

I have refrained from adding sermon materials and moralizing in these stories. The Spirit of God will reveal His truth to the reader according to each one's needs. Come with me; let's walk together where God also joined me on the journey.

CHAPTER ONE

WE RECEIVE A CALL

When I entered the pastoral ministry, my mind overflowed with concepts from seminary about what type a leader I ought to be. Would I be a manager, player, coach, shepherd, or other fad titles? In my heart I knew I was a knight in shining armor, going into the kingdom of my Lord to do battle and subdue alien rebels. I wanted to anticipate problems and solve them before they even came to the surface. When there was a challenge, I wanted to resolve it for my Lord. My goal was to protect the King's interest and keep His people from harm.

If I did well, and removed hindrances to church growth for my King, God would reward me and the church would grow.

Upon graduating from seminary, I was eager to pastor a church. It had been my dream since high school. I considered becoming an associate pastor to gain more insight into this new job, but my preparation and dream was to be a pastor now, not later.

Annual "District Superintendent Day" at the seminary is always an exciting -- if not a stressful day -- for the graduating seniors. They meet the DS's responsible for finding the right person to fill an open church. Many churches had reputations as "an opportunity" for the right person to bring the dead to life. Sometimes the only qualification for the "right person" was, "Is he breathing and standing upright?"

At "District Superintendent Day" the administrators from across the denomination meet with the graduating seniors for lunch. After lunch they mingle informally. Each graduating senior who desires to pastor in a local church, talks to district superintendents supervising areas of the country where one might be interested in being a pastor.

My wife, Cindy, is from Omaha, Nebraska, a city of half a million people. I was from Plummer, Pennsylvania, home of two hundred and fifty people, near the "large" city of Oil City, PA, with a of population twenty thousand. Of course, my perspective of what was small and what was large changed after attending college in Oklahoma City and seminary in Kansas City. Since I felt more comfortable in a town of twenty thousand, my desire was to start in what I now considered a 'small' town of about 20,000 people. We really had no inclination of where to pastor, but we hoped to be near one set of parents, Nebraska or Ohio.

I had not thought through this population thing. I consider myself a small town boy: twenty thousand isn't big. That led to my blunder with the Nebraska District

Superintendent. I asked around until I found someone who directed me to the DS from Nebraska. When he was free, I introduced myself and said to him, "My wife's parents are in Omaha First Church." He recognized her maiden name and knew the family. I told him I was interested in coming to Nebraska. He tried to determine if I could be content in a small community. He knew Cindy was from Omaha, a metropolis. He asked, "How big of a city do you want to start in?"

I said, "Oh, I'm from a small town of only 20,000 people, so I am willing to pastor in a town that small."

The man's face bloated as he tried to hold his laughter. Finally he could not hold it any longer. He laughed in my face! His expression was one of total disbelief. What had I said wrong?

The superintendent put his arm around my shoulder and said, "In Nebraska we only have two towns over 20,000. I don't think the pastors in those towns are ready to move." With that and a chuckle to himself, he dismissed me from his presence and I am sure from his mind forever. I thought, "I am so dumb. Why did I say twenty thousand people?" I was going to have to be more careful.

My understanding was that the District Superintendent would take my name, pray about it, present my resume to a church board, the church board would interview me and the congregation would vote if there was mutual interest. However, District Superintendents do not all work that way. Maybe none of them followed my idea. For instance, one man told me, "I don't have anything right now, but whenever another District Superintendent calls you, call me right away to see if I have anything available."

Clever way to operate, I thought. Do not rely on your own judgment of the man. First, see if someone else wants him. Of course, I am sure the District Superintendent was separating those who expressed interest from those who were really interested, but did not want to pastor in a state with cities hours apart,

In spite of all the interviews and resumes, the time-honored method of placement in a church is who you know. Two years earlier, after my first year of seminary, the Philadelphia District had a combined camp program with the Washington District. An in-service training job with the combined districts was arranged through the seminary for a married couple. The couple would work in the various age group camps, in the camp meeting, and supply pulpits on the weekend.

Cindy and I tried to do something special in our summers. I sold books for Southwestern Company one summer. . We went to Israel another summer. When DS Reverend Hutton came to the seminary to interview interested applicants for the camp job, we thought working in camps and preaching in the area would be fun. Besides, I had never seen an ocean.

We made an appointment with Reverend Hutton. He was looking for general helpers in the camp, who would fill in where needed. In the weeks with no camps, I would help with the remodeling and the constant upkeep that is required around a campground.

Cindy and I had been married two years, but I still thought of us as newlyweds. I had a question because of other camps I had attended and worked as a teen. In those camps married counselors were separated and stayed in the dorms with the campers. Where would we be staying? Rev. Hutton told us Washington, D.C. First Church had made its cabin available to us except during the ten day camp meeting. During camp meeting we would stay in the camp motel. Well, exactly what will we do? I explained, "I would rather not be housed with a group of boys all week long."

With very clear insight, Rev. Hutton said, "Except in emergencies, you will sleep in your cottage with your wife in a double bed." That settled it. We went.

The internship was a wonderful experience. The camp was not prepared when we first arrived, and I did carpentry and plumbing. I learned new skills and had wonderful fellowship with the men and women who were volunteering their time. Some of the workers were retired pastors, and I was like a sponge listening to their stories.

The camp workers also learned I had more energy than ability. They were building a new dining hall. Volunteers came when they had a day or two to give. Two retired men were there frequently to work. The full time caretaker and I rounded out the crew. It was important to get the dining hall finished and soon, because they could not start camp until the building inspector approved the building. The date of the first youth camp was fast approaching.

The dry wall was up, and I was helping the electrician

pull wires. It was hot in the attic space, where I was walking on the rafters. I missed a rafter and came down through the newly hung dry wall. Both of my legs hung to the hips through the ceiling. One of the hard working volunteers said, "Must be that seminary guy. I don't recognize the legs."

The summer held lots of variety. I had hoped to be involved in the planning sessions but that didn't work out since it was done before we arrived. However, we made friends with teens who wrote to us for a couple of years. On weekends, Cindy and I drove to various churches throughout Pennsylvania, Maryland, and New Jersey.

If churches where I was to speak were close enough to the camp, we drove on Sunday to the community. Pastors on vacation, and those brave enough to give me an opportunity, opened their pulpits to me. I was nervous when it came to preaching. I had not spoken to large groups and had just a few sermons that I had prepared during seminary.

One June Sunday, I was in a large, beautiful sanctuary. The pastor was gone. A carefully dressed and serous looking man led me to a room beside the platform.

"Young man, our pastor always dismisses us at twelve noon," the man said with some sternness.

I gave him an innocent look and asked, "What time will I start preaching?"

He said, "Around twenty minutes after eleven."

With as straight a face as I could muster I asked him, "Sir, what will I do? My longest sermon is only twenty minutes."

Quickly he raised his hands and responded, "Oh that's okay. That's okay!"

Even though the benediction was before noon, it must have been okay. They had me back three other Sundays and even the wonderful pastor, Reverend Warren Hollaway, was present when not busy with district activities.

The summer camp experience was at the end of my first year of seminary. By my last year in seminary and the District Superintendents' meeting with graduating seniors, Reverend Hutton had moved from Maryland to Illinois. I greeted him at the meeting. He told me he would keep me in mind for a church.

Many things were on my mind in the final semester of school. Will I get a call? If I get calls from more than one church, where would God want me to go? How would I know if it was the right choice? Sometime a knight can be powerfully insecure.

Then on top of that, Cindy and I were expecting our first child. The doctor said the baby was due July 1 or the last week of June. I wished he had said later. Cindy was not sure she wanted to move before the baby was born. She was not sure we would be able to pack the house and move when she was eight months pregnant. Mostly she did not want to change doctors.

One day after class, I talked to one of my professors about Cindy's feelings. He assured me that they had moved when his wife was pregnant, and it all worked out. "Let God take care of it."

That night the knight in shining armor came home and told his princess everything would be all right. God would take care of her and God would not lead us anywhere that would hurt us. Now would that not make any wife feel better? At least she said, "We will wait and see."

In March, Reverend Hutton called. "There is a church I want you to look at, preach for them, and see if you like the area." We agreed to go the next weekend.

It was a five-hour drive to Illinois and by the time we got there, it was raining hard. About three miles from town a dog ran across the road in the blinding rain, and I could not avoid hitting it. Not exactly how I wanted to start my first meeting at my first church. Was this an omen of our ministry?

That was the only disappointment in my interview weekend. The people greeted us warmly. They took us to see the parsonage in the rain, late Saturday night. It was a Sears Roebuck mail order house. They showed us its vast rooms, the large archways, the high ceilings, and they explained it was cold upstairs because the heat was off. After touring the parsonage, they took us to the home of a delightful elderly couple who would become our close friends.

The next day I preached my best sermon. Every preacher has at least one, but that became my only trial sermon. When the worship service closed, the church board secretary came to me. She asked, "When will you tell the DS if you are coming or not?"

I replied that Reverend Hutton would be in touch

with them, for I knew the congregation had to vote first. He had to approve, and then I could say if we were coming. Nevertheless, most of all, Cindy and I were going to pray about going to Carlinville.

In a few days, Reverend Hutton called. The congregation had extended a unanimous call. Sixteen had voted. Would I come? We had already prayed. Yes, we would come.

"Will you start now? Drive to Carlinville on weekends? Then move after graduation?" He explained it would only be two months.

I wanted to say "yes", but explained why I thought it was too much to travel those weekends for two months. I was still working part time as a janitor and going to school. Cindy, being great with child, could not be racing back and forth ten hours every weekend. He understood and said to let the church know when we would move.

The day after graduation, we moved out of a ten-foot wide mobile home and were able to sell it for the same price we paid for it. Housing during seminary years had cost us only lot rent, plus heat and electricity. That was as prosperous as we would be for many years.

Knights are not to be prosperous, just adventurous. They go where they are needed. We were on our way.

CHAPTER TWO

GOD'S CARE

Leaving a mobile home with its limited space and moving into a huge house was a pure joy. Cindy had a great deal of fun planning a baby's room and unpacking everything. We had very little furniture, but the money from the sale of our mobile home provided the solution to that problem. We bought a dining room table, six chairs, a huge one piece china cabinet, and a bedroom suite.

Experience is a good teacher. It was a mistake to buy the one piece china cabinet. The dining room table is perfect for us. It is a six feet long oval table with two twenty inch extensions. That first dining room was fifteen by eighteen feet, bigger than some garages. It had large arches coming into it from the other rooms. I guess we figured our first parsonage would probably be our smallest, and the beautiful table would grace any house.

The matching china cabinet is six feet tall and five feet wide, also beautiful. Somehow it didn't occur to me that at sixty years of age, I would not be as strong as I was at age twenty five. Experience is a good teacher.

⬥⬥⬥⬥

Kansas City had named streets and numbered houses. We moved to Carlinville, Illinois, where our ministry would be mostly rural. Mail was delivered to rural route one, rural route two, and rural route three. This was before the days of 911 and the requirement that all house numbers have to be displayed on the mail boxes or houses.

It was a challenge to visit someone's house. I first had to locate the county road and then the township road and then the lane with a familiar land mark to local people, but not to a new pastor, like I was. So it was with considerable luck and ecstasy that I found church members.

Learning to find a specific family in the country was a chore. How I now empathized with the drivers who got lost in Kansas City traffic. I got lost as soon as I got off the main highway.

Shortly after we arrived in town, Cindy and I were being shown how the roads were laid out. Kathy, one of the high school students who attended our church, volunteered for the task of introducing us to the area. Kathy really cared about people. As an adult she became a missionary doctor with ability and confidence; but not that night as a teenager.

Along the route she intended to use, the road was blocked. The fire department was engaging a fire. Fire hoses stretched from a stream across the road to the tanker truck, so we could not use that familiar road. Our guide was not deterred. She was sure she could find the way. All we had to do was drive to another section road and follow it and we would eventually come back out on the high way. An hour later, in the dark, we finally came to a marked, familiar road and returned home.

I had been told if a woman was pregnant and near her due date, go for a ride on a bumpy road. After an evening of calling on a family that lived on a bumpy country farm road, Cindy woke me and said, "I just had a funny feeling that I've never had before."

We were to call the doctor when labor started. Is this how labor starts? It was midnight. We called the doctor. The doctor's wife said, "Call again in two hours." Two hours later the funny feelings were more frequent. "Call again in two hours." At four o'clock I called again. The doctor's wife received the call. She asked cheerfully, "How is she doing?"

I was so scared. How could anyone be cheerful at four in the morning? Just then Cindy had a contraction. It wasn't a funny feeling anymore. She screamed like the farmers calling the hogs. "Is that her?" asked the now not so calm doctor's wife."

"Yes, Ma'am," I said.

"You better get her over to the hospital right away. The doctor will meet you."

Fortunately it was only four blocks to the hospital. Unfortunately it was one hundred feet to the car. It became a "hurry up" and "wait" process.

"Wait." Pause for a contraction. "Okay, we can go now," Cindy said. We would take a couple steps. A contraction would come, "Wait!" she would scream. I was sure the neighbors would call the police that someone was being beaten in the parsonage yard.

Finally we got to the car and I drove to the hospital. It was another five hours until Boyd was born. I don't know what the rush was! And it wasn't late June. It wasn't the first week of July. It was August 8th. Yes. God did know when we could move.

The move was also evidence of God's providential care. Cindy's blood was checked each week during the final trimester of her pregnancy. We were told each time everything was normal. The doctor anticipated no problems.

In the first week in our new community, Cindy went to her new doctor, a general practitioner. One person drew us aside after church and discouraged us from choosing this particular doctor. It was known in town that the doctor occasionally admitted himself to the psychiatric hospital suffering from what was then called "shell shock." It is now called post traumatic stress. We liked the doctor as a person and chose to let him be our family doctor and care for Cindy through the pregnancy. There were no obstetricians available as in the larger city we had left.

Like the previous physician, this doctor also drew blood. At her next appointment he told her the blood test revealed she had a condition known as the RH factor. It meant that Cindy's blood was building antibodies against the baby's blood. To protect future pregnancies, it would be necessary for her to have a specially prepared medication. This would need to be administered within twenty-four hours of giving birth. The doctor made arrangements for the injection and Cindy was fine.

My Uncle Bogue and Aunt Eula Mae lost a baby due to the RH factor. My uncle sobbed in our home over their loss. I was about seven years old and it is the earliest I observed someone else's sorrow and felt hurt with them. God knew when we needed to move and He knew the doctor we needed. He moved us three hundred miles to put us with the right doctor. Bigger is not always better.

⚬⚬⚬

The congregation treated us graciously but they were concerned. Previous pastors had stayed as short as a year. Of course, one potential problem in any job is salary. That was why some of the previous pastors moved to other places. It was a valid concern.

The most the church thought they could afford to pay a pastor was sixty-five dollars a week. The District Superintendent said the district would supplement the salary with another twenty. I did not ask for the additional money but he extended it. I told him we would do our best not to need it beyond one year. I was also determined that I would live on what we received. I intended to be a full time pastor and not work a second job.

That was a new concept to the congregation. At first, when we arrived, we were asked if I was going to drive school bus or teach school. Others had, and they were good pastors. I felt if I was on the King's business, He would take care of me. And God did. At times we gave into the offering plate enough so they could pay our salary. We had no school bills, no car payment and the sale of the mobile home paid for the furniture.

God provided for us and though others would do differently, there are two principles that I have chosen to live by. The first is to return to God twenty percent of my income. We were challenged to do that by a retired pastor in a youth service when in college. It really laid our finances in God's lap. We were four thousand dollars in debt to the school and had only a two dollar an hour job. Cindy and I agreed to double tithe and we left college and seminary debt free.

The second principle established my priorities. God is first in my life but my family is before my job as a minster. I do not want my wife and family to feel they are second to my occupation. For example, when we sold the mobile home that had been our seminary housing, we could have bought a new car. I need a dependable car, I reasoned.

When I asked an experienced pastor, should I buy a car or furniture, he advised, "You will always have a car payment. It is part of the cost of doing business. Keep your wife happy." So instead of buying a new car, we bought the furniture and have never been sorry -- except the one piece china cabinet is too heavy. Over the years we bought several new and used cars for ministry, but the furniture still is lovely. My wife has been a comfortable hostess. Purchasing the furniture illustrated to her she was first.

Another reason I believe God has taken care of us

financially is because we pray about almost every purchase. God's direction to one car was very specific. Deciding what car to buy has always been a challenge for me. I drove clunkers that were worn out when I got them. I have driven cars purchased at the police auction. I bought my first car with no reverse, but I had no intentions of going backwards anyway.

While driving to seminary, the same route each day, I noticed a car, a Lincoln Continental that was never moved. The tires were turned to the curb and leaves had gathered under it. I prayed for God's guidance in buying a car, and the Lincoln kept coming to my mind. I decided to stop and ask about it.

I approached the house closest to the car. A man in his sixties answered my knock on the door. He was unhappy to be disturbed from his sleep, but surprised when I asked him about the car.

The Lincoln belonged to his wife who had died one year earlier. The car was ten years old, and he asked me to make an offer. Promising to find how much it was worth, I went on to class.

Later, I looked at the car more closely and discovered it was spotless. The Lincoln was burgundy with white leather upholstery. I described the car to the loan officer at the bank. The bank didn't keep values on cars that old. I found one Lincoln on a used car lot that was about the same age but the inside was a disaster. It also had nearly a hundred thousand miles on it which was twice the miles as the other car. The used car salesman wanted a thousand dollars for the trashed car.

I called about the spotless Lincoln and told the man his car was worth more than a thousand dollars, and I would not be able to buy it. He asked me, "How much money do you have?"

"I have three hundred dollars," I told him.

When I went to pay him, he said, "You can have the car for two hundred and fifty dollars." You can imagine my surprise and praise to God. We drove the Lincoln during the last year of seminary and two years of our first pastorate. Mileage was poor but the ride was great and the investment low. It served us well

Several years later, enquiring about a new car at a dealership, I was reminded of that Lincoln and God's direction. The salesman pitched, "You better take it today because it will soon be gone." I said, "I am going home and pray about it." His reply indicated he had not enjoyed much of God's miraculous supply. "God doesn't care which car you buy," he said. O yes, God does care. He has the car picked out for me before I ask.

A pastor in farm country doesn't have to worry about food. People brought us garden produce in season. I thought I would try my hand at gardening. I dug up a small plot and told Cindy we would give away everything that grew on one side of the garden. It was the Lord's. Everything that grew on the other side would be for our own use. It spite of my best intentions, we ended up eating God's side. Our side did not come up.

One day I was calling on potential church people. I stopped to see Ford, the brother of one of the woman in the congregation. I didn't know him, only his sister, but after a few minutes of visiting with Ford, I learned he was a hog farmer. He offered to give us a hog to put in our freezer. We didn't have a freezer, but I went home and told Cindy of the offer. Cindy was teaching piano lessons to the neighborhood children and thought she could afford a freezer.

In small towns, credit is a lot easier with local merchants unless you show you are not to be trusted. Even the meter cop took the nickels drivers left on their windshields to put them in the expired meters. People just trusted each other.

If I needed something for the plumbing but wasn't sure which piece I needed, the clerk would send several parts home with me and say, "Bring back the ones you don't use." He never wrote down a list of what I had taken and I never paid for anything until I returned with the unused items. The local hardware sold freezers. He sold us a freezer on credit, no interest.

Leo and Amy Colyar said they would pay for cutting and wrapping the meat. I hadn't even thought of that. God was really taking care of us.

"But God," I asked, "who do you expect to kill that hog? Who is going to gut it and hang it? I am a city boy." I am not sure how God felt, but I was relieved to find out that the butcher did those things and it was all included in the price. All I had to do was get the hog the twenty-five miles from the farmer to the butcher. I didn't know for sure if pigs like to ride in Lincolns, but I was sure some of those pigs I had seen couldn't be easy to get into the car. The farmer said I could use his pickup truck with the cattle confiner and it would be no problem.

When the pickup was backed up to the gate of the hog pen, Ford asked, "Which one do you want?" I said that I didn't know. The farmer said, "Pick one out."

I said, "Ford, I don't know pigs. Since you do and you are giving it away, I would be pleased if you picked the pig you want me to have."

He chased a pig out of the herd and into the truck and said, "There you go Preacher."

"Ford, how can you afford to give me a pig? I know pig farmers are barely making it."

He responded, "Preacher, I can give that hog away and come out better than paying for feed." And because of the poor farm prices he was right.

With joy and gratitude I jumped in his truck and carefully delivered my pig to the butcher. The man's first words were, "That is really a nice looking hog, young man." God and His people have taken care of me and fed my family. By what He gives me, I am sure God is not a vegetarian and certainly not kosher.

Chapter Three

WEDDINGS

Regardless of circumstances, my first goal was to serve God. He was generous with us. Like Peter, in Matthew 14, I didn't want to sit in the boat during the storm, I wanted to walk on water and be part of the miracle. I wanted to bring the part of the kingdom where I lived into submission to the King.

I heard an insurance manager telling one of his agents, "Take care of the people, and the people will take care of you." I was determined to pastor God's people.

How would I get them to the place where they needed or wanted a pastor? I was to bury the dead, marry the willing, and dedicate the babies; but no one wanted to die, and the church had no young waiting to be married. People that don't marry don't dedicate babies. I could call on my entire congregation in one week with a little effort. I did that occasionally just for the challenge.

Mostly, I worked on sermons. Frantically, I worked on sermons. Seminary deadlines were only a drop in the bucket compared to preaching twice a week and conducting a Bible study on Wednesday. Mercifully, I have forgotten most of those sermons. Whenever I found one of them tucked away in my files, I feel sorry for those patient people.

A couple of the board members asked if they could speak to me "Critically, but we think, helpfully."

"Of course you can." I was terrified inside. Did they find out about the dog I had hit in the rain? Surely they had not discovered my secret after all this time. Were they going to ask me to work harder? I would but I didn't know how. I worked every day already.

"We think you are too hard on the children, Pastor. We are sure if you had children junior age you would understand and not be so quick to discipline them. We just thought you would like to know our feelings." I was grateful to them. I was grateful that they told me. Grateful they didn't know about the dog.

⬥⬥⬥

Gradually the new people, to whom I extended a welcome, came to church. People did want to know the King. They did want to serve Him as part of a community of believers. In small towns people don't make changes as easily as they do in more populated areas. People often stay in the same church, just as they have lived on the same farm for generations. They don't change churches, even if they do not attend regularly. They do want the church when there is a need.

One evening a young couple came to the door. They

were about twenty years old. His aunt had told me they were coming. They wanted to get married. This would be my first wedding.

I asked all the questions on my premarital counseling questionnaire but one. That's just too personal I reasoned. The next week they were married at the church altar. Six months later they had their first child. That was the question I had neglected. I never would again.

After the baby was born, the young man wanted free. He wanted to be a hippy, like they had been before they got married. His plan was pot and free sex. She wanted to settle down and have a stable home. I felt sad for her. She wanted a loving home, and I had contributed to her problem.

When people think of the work of the pastor, they think, "hitching" and "ditching"; weddings and funerals. But in small towns with numerous churches, a pastor will never wear out his hitching and ditching suit. Some think that the pastor's job is to marry everyone with a desire to get married, and they send couples to the parsonage.

One afternoon a middle aged man, a young teen, and a boy walked onto the parsonage porch. The neighbor next to the church had directed them to our home. The man looked to be in his thirties and asked, "Would you marry us?" Several people were looking out the open widows of the car that was parked by the curb. I asked him, "Who is getting married?"

He responded, "Us," and pointed to the young girl that had come up on the porch beside him.

I asked if they had a marriage license. He handed me

an envelope. I invited them into the parsonage. As the young boy ran to the car, he hollered, "He's a gonna' do it. He's a gonna do it."

It was then that I looked closely at the car. It was already decorated with white crepe paper, and shaving cream spelled out, "Just Married." Tin cans were tied to the bumper.

"I believe we need to talk about this," was my opening remark as I looked at the wedding license. It revealed his age to be thirty four and hers was sixteen.

"We know all about the Christian life. There is no need to talk," he responded.

I attempted to give them some guidance. "There's a lot to know about life and each other besides the Christian life." I hoped to get them to change their minds about an immediate wedding.

He responded, "I have known her all week. We know all we need to know about each other. Are you going to marry us or not?"

"I'm sorry I can't marry you without counseling, and that requires time. I believe you will find it helpful." He was not to be put off. "Do you know someone who will marry us? We have been to every church, and the pastors are all on vacation." I knew that was true because I had been doing hospital calls for the other pastors. When a town only has three Protestant and two Catholic congregations, it is possible for all to be gone at the same time.

He continued, "The judge said he didn't have time to marry us." I knew it would only take a few minutes for a civil ceremony, but even the judge was sitting this one out.

I didn't know anyone who could marry them immediately, but again assured them it would be good to have some marriage counseling while they waited. I hoped the neighbors weren't watching as they ran to the car and drove down the street with the tin cans bouncing off the pavement and shaving cream announcing, "Just Married".

The next week I saw them. He was riding a bicycle, and she was running a couple steps behind. They didn't even have a bicycle built for two.

Chapter Four

GOSSIP AND BLESSINGS

Gossip is always a curse. I tried to keep our church free of it. It was exciting to hear news, but not when it was gossip that was cutting someone down. In spite of my good intentions, I almost became part of the gossip trail.

Phil and Deloris were in their in their late thirties and the second marriage for each. She had one daughter who lived with them. Phil had let Deloris know he wanted to have a baby. She did not agree.

Our church nursery attendant had told me that we would soon have another baby and it was Phil and Deloris who were expecting. I was elated for them. After all, the nursery attendant should know.

A few days later, I was at their home and noted Deloris was wearing a loose duster. She must be pregnant. When I prayed for my people in their homes, I included their personal concerns.. I thought to myself, "I should remember their baby when I pray today." After admiring their pond and yard in front of their modest home, I read from the Word of God and prayed. I concluded prayer with, "Bless the baby that is coming to this home."

The next week Deloris knocked at our door. I was gone but Cindy invited her in and they visited briefly. Then Deloris asked Cindy, "Does your husband think I am pregnant?"

Cindy responded, "I don't know. Why?"

Deloris explained. "Well, last week when Pastor prayed for us, he prayed for the coming baby. After he left, Phil looked at me with great joy in his eyes and asked, 'Honey, Are you pregnant?'

"Cindy, I am not pregnant. Phil is upset because I am not pregnant."

I was glad that I wasn't home to hear my mistake. Sometimes a knight should keep his mouth shut.

⁂

Pastors can also be the target of gossip.

The nearest church of our denomination was twenty miles away; this was the first pastoral assignment for Reverend Harold and Janet Clay. They had a new baby, like Cindy and I. Harold had grown up in a parsonage, but I had not. His dad was a district superintendent in a distant state. I respected Harold's advice because he always had an answer while I was still trying to figure out the question. We became friends

We got together for fellowship a couple of times a month. The four of us would play Rook. There were certain precautions we took before playing games in his town. He tightly closed the doors. He pulled the shades until no light could be seen, and he moved the table to the back of the house. "Why are we doing all this?" I asked.

"It might ruin us if some know we play cards." I wondered how they could think badly of their pastor playing Rook.

Some of his church members walked the shallow river in their underwear in daylight. They probed under the banks for the large catfish, stroking their bellies, which paralyzed them. Then they could be guided into gunny sacks and hauled to shore.

It was a double standard. We weren't gambling. We weren't drinking alcohol. They could walk the river in their underwear and that was considered normal but we were considered publicans for playing cards.

⊠⊠⊠

However, keeping the gossip out was important to trust and a sense of unity in the church. People would come to church and get blessed.

One of our favorite ladies who would get blessed was Miss Patterson. She was elderly and crippled, and lived in one of the three nursing homes of Carlinville. I don't know how the small town had so many old people. I guess because none of them were anxious to die. They wanted to go to heaven, but not right now.

Miss Paterson loved to come to church. The previous two pastors would not bring her, because they didn't want to be responsible for her. We made it a habit of driving Miss Patterson to church when it wasn't icy. When she came to church, glory came on the services. The testimonies were better. The singing was better. I preached better. I loved Miss Patterson to worship with us.

There were times I wondered if my predecessors were not wiser than I by leaving her in the nursing home on Sunday mornings.

She would stand during worship and shout "Glory!" She would raise her arms and shout, "Glory!" That was good. She would wave her upraised arms from side to side. That was okay. She would grasp the back of the pew in front of her and jump up and down shouting, "Glory, Glory, Glory." That was okay too. But the day she raised her arms and jumped up and down at the same time, was the day everyone in attendance quit breathing and only she shouted, "Glory!" She was unsteady and used a walker that enclosed her except when she was in the church pew. We were afraid she would fall down and break a hip.

After the service a member drew me aside and said, "Pastor, you just got to quit bringing Miss Patterson to church. If she falls, you're responsible. If she breaks a leg, you're responsible. Pastor, I just don't want us to be responsible." Every time I took her from the nursing home, I was required to sign that I would watch over her and make sure she got back.

To the nervous member I responded, "I know you mean well. But Miss Patterson has no other family. The Church is her life. As long as she wants to come, I am going to bring her." As a representative of the King, on His business miles from His palace, Miss Patterson kept the joy of being a knight alive.

Chapter Five

THE CHURCH GOT STONED

It was only a few months until our building was crowded. This was the usual cycle for the Church. The history was an overflowing building, followed by discouragement and loss of attendance, because nothing was done to provide more space. The finances were limited. We were paying our obligations to the district and general church. This was new for the church, and the folks were proud to be doing their part to reach the lost in the nations of the world, but a few complained about sending "all that money" away.

If I were going to be a good representative of the King, I needed to get the congregation excited about what God was doing for them. One focus was the building. What could we do about our building? My district superintendent said to me immediately after I accepted the church, "The district will help you get a building." But Reverend Hutton had been in the hospital from the very first Sunday I was in my church. He had an aneurism, near his heart, and we expected a long convalescence. I didn't want to trouble him.

The twenty dollars that had been promised from the district had not been coming due to the DS's illness. The church was paying the full salary, waiting to see what would happen when the district superintended was back in his office. Although the aneurism was bad for Reverend Hutton, God says, "All things work together for good." Now it was clear to us, the church could pay a salary without the district's help. If he had been able to tell the district treasure to send the money, the local church would have accepted. Instead, they saw they could do it on their own.

⚔

Our church building was only forty by sixty feet. There were four small rooms in the corners. Over the entry was a balcony. On the other end was a room over the pulpit. Cindy worked with the children in the Sunday school. They came on their own or were picked up by church members. Children filled all the rooms. The adults met together in the worship area. The balcony and the room in one back corner were open to the sanctuary. Occasionally paper would rain down on the adults and it was noisy. In the other corner, to the back, was the nursery. How could we reach more people, so we could build a building? We couldn't even start another adult Sunday school class?

A church was disbanding fifty miles away. I had driven by the building and noticed a mobile home on the same lot. It had been used as a parsonage. The district treasure told me it was available. We could use it, if we paid the expense of moving the trailer. The district insurance covered it when it was setting on a permanent location, but not in transit.

The Church Board approved moving it to be used. I called a mobile home sales office. Their crew would move it but buying insurance for a one time move on a trailer we didn't own was difficult. Finally, I was able to locate an insurer in a distant state whose company would consider insuring the move.

"How far are you going to move it?" The agent asked me. I assumed he was filling out a form.

"Fifty miles," I said.

"When are you going to move it?"

"Tomorrow," I answered.

Then he asked, "How do I know the payment will be made before you move the trailer?"

"Sir," I answered, "I am on the King's business. I will mail the payment whether the trailer is moved safely or we have damage." And I did.

❖

One of our high school students painted a sign and hung it on the building. The sign was inspirational. "Don't just watch us grow, come grow with us." The trailer had enough space for an opening exercise and three classes. The kids got to sing children's songs and take leadership in their own programs.

Though we ran electricity to the new facility, we

had no water or sewage. It was a temporary solution to a growing church. The children went to the church building to use the rest rooms. Occasionally, a child would manage to unlock the restroom door in the temporary facility and use the toilet that had no water in it. A week later, in hot weather, the trailer seriously needed fresh air.

The restrooms in the church building seemed like an afterthought. The doors opened into the foyer. Evidently the designer felt that if restrooms were necessary, he would make them as small as possible. The men's and women's rest rooms were the same size --two and half by three feet. The sink extended over the toilet. If a person planned to sit, the bending process had to begin before closing the door. People who seemed to have won their spiritual victory could be heard cussing six feet away..

The mobile unit relieved our sanctuary Sunday school noise problem and gave us space to grow. Something still needed to be done about a permanent building. I talked to a local contractor, arranged a meeting with an architect, had some preliminary drawings done, then it all came back to money. "We don't have any money. Why are you trying to get us all excited about it? You'll just go off and leave us with a big debt."

⨳⨳

Our current building was located on three lots. It had once been a swamp. A ditch ran on the south edge of the property. It caused much grief, especially in the winter. Cars slid into the ditch that was six feet deep. I talked to the councilman several times about getting it leveled. He must have thought he was at church, because his line was the same as my church board, "We don't have any money to fill in that ditch."

I asked him if the city would supply the pipe if the church supplied the dirt. We needed the parking space. I told him how much of an eye sore it was. All the trash that blew across town went into our ditch. I also told him it really was dangerous for "ditch divers". He agreed there was a problem but made no promises.

The Christian church was excavating for a new sanctuary. The contractor was hauling the dirt out of town. I reasoned it would save them money to haul it two blocks to our property. I asked the contractor if he could haul the dirt to our church lot. He dumped load after load where the proposed building would go. The area was lower than the street and the architect had said we should raise the building site to street level.

Before Sunday, we had close to forty loads of dirt dumped on the church yard. There were shocked expressions on the faces of our people when they arrived at church. I explained that the dirt was free, and even if it took ten years to build, we would still use the dirt. The explanation calmed some of them down, especially when they heard it was free dirt.

Meanwhile, the councilman was alarmed. He saw all the dirt next to the ditch and was afraid it would be filled in without the pipe. On Monday there was three hundred feet of twenty-four inch concrete pipe in the ditch, and they brought their own dirt and covered it up.

Before the next election the councilman called me.

"Reverend, you remember how hard I worked to get the city to fill in the ditch. Now you tell all your people to vote for me Tuesday."

"I thought you were running unopposed." I said.

"I am, but you never know. Somebody might have a write in campaign."

I wish I had had the nerve to tell him what I thought. "You did nothing to get that ditch filled in. I hounded you and hounded you, and finally you thought I was doing it, so you requested it done. You ought to be opposed, and you ought to be defeated." The knight can be elegant in his own head.

⬡⬡⬡

The cost of our proposed building was more than the conservative farmers could imagine. They were each in debt more than the cost of the proposed structure and they didn't have enough pooled faith for a church. What else could we do? If a congregation can't build the whole thing at once, start somewhere.

A man in his seventies and his paralysis stricken wife started attending. In spite of illness, they had lots of life and faith. He was still working. She had overcome a stroke, regained some speech, and walked with assistance.

This precious man had forms to pour decorative stone. He said he would provide the material if we would provide the labor. I figured how much stone it would take to cover our present building and one twice as large. I divided it by the forms available. It would take forty days to make eight thousand bricks. Forty days was a test in the Bible. Would we meet the test?

The forms produced two, three inch thick stones, each fifteen inches long. We decided on three earth tone colors. The gravel was river grade and made a beautiful face when fractured as designed.

Ben Strode, was a public school teacher with summers free -- except for sports practices, EMT, fire department and caring for the yards of shut ins. He agreed to lead a few workers and I would also take a group. Each team would go every other day. We would work six days a week. The plan was to take the stone out that had been poured the day before, clean the molds, oil the molds, and pour. It was simple on paper. A team of three or four could do it in two hours. It was eleven miles from the church to the work site.

It only took a few days for me to realize every other day was not going to work. I resigned myself to the fact that I was going to have to go every day. Cindy, with an infant, would join me when she could. Others got discouraged, tired, and gave up, but I kept at it. Ben had a big heart and good intentions, but many had demands on him, and he could not commit three days a week to making stone. Leo and Amy Colyar, elderly church members, drove to the work site several times, but it was young people's work.

First, the twenty pound blocks were removed from the forms and stacked. Every day they had to be carried a little farther. The forms had to be cleaned and oiled. Next, the cement mixer was filled by measured shovel loads of sand, gravel, and cement. The sand and gravel also got farther away from the cement mixer every day. A cup of dye and five gallons of water completed the recipe. When the mixture was right, the mixer would be dumped into a wheel barrow then scooped with two quart pitchers into the molds. The molds were tapped gently on the sides to get rid of air pockets and floated with a trowel. A divider was laid on top of the stone and the cement left to dry.

Each morning it was evident if something had been forgotten the day before. If the cement was not added to the sand and gravel, the stone would break in your hands as it was carried. Since each batch filled twelve molds, I knew right away twenty four stones were useless. Sometimes the color would not be right and I knew someone had not added the dye to the batch. I asked myself who ran the mixer yesterday. Who fed the dye? Who scraped the molds?

Often I had only one answer. I was the one who forgot as I hurried between the stations of sand, gravel, dye, mixer and water. I was the guilty party. I and a junior boy or two had come, and I didn't trust them to do it right

When about 6,000 stones had been prepared, one of the church board members asked, "Why don't we quit for a while? We can do it some other time"

"Lord," I complained with pride, "You know most of the others have already quit, and they just want me to quit too so they won't feel so guilty. I'll see it out to the end." I empathized with Nehemiah battling the excuses of why the walls could not be built.

We tried different ways to make pouring stone fun. We had a bike hike with the stone site as the destination. We had a hot dog roast at the farm, but we had to pour stone before we ate. Like Moses it took us forty days. We had been to the wilderness and back. We overcame the rebellion of tired bodies and naysayers. The stone was finally all poured. I was proud to be a knight in service to the King.

We had one final party. We had a stone moving party. Two flat bed trucks were supplied by farmers. We formed an assembly line, and loaded the trucks. We moved eight thousand stones to the church property, and set them around the building. Everyone was excited. Everyone wanted to have a part. Folks moved stones, fixed lunch, drove truck, or just cheered, but the stones moved. We made two trips with the trucks, we worked all day, but we got them moved. The Church got stoned but we were all sober. Surely now the congregation would say, "We can do anything."

CHAPTER SIX

PLANS CAN BACKFIRE

Miss Isel Goodell lived two short blocks from the church and faithfully attended. She was a former piano teacher in her late sixties and we fell in love with her. Sometimes she would baby sit for us if we took Boyd to her house. The house was only two rooms, but she was proud of it.

Isel's mother had worked and lived in the local orphanage causing Isel to say, with a hint of mystery, "I grew up in an orphanage." She gave that reason as why she never wanted to live in one of the beautiful new nursing homes in our area. The nursing homes, or assisted living, sounded like institutions to her.

Isel wore a leg brace because she had polio as a child. Her legs were weak and undependable so we worried about her walking to church. The first few months I was her pastor, she always rebuked me when I stopped to offer her a ride. "As long as I got one good leg, God means me to use it," she would say sternly. I would drive on questioning her wisdom.

In the winter, she yielded to our persistence, and agreed to let the Strode family pick her up for church. With her strong sense of independence, she did not give in to a battered leg. Somehow she overcame that strong self will, and allowed herself to ride to church for the next summer.

Ben Strode, Isel's volunteer chauffer, also was the Sunday School Superintendent, adult Sunday school teacher, choir director, worship leader, piano player, organist, and the reason the church had survived through the ups and downs of spiritual drought and seasons of renewal. Miss Goodell would hobble home without waiting for us if Ben or I took too long in a meeting, after a service. Ben and I had several guilt trips. She never complained, but we knew we had neglected her.

Ben's personality was a gift from God to our church. He kept the services fun and alive. One Christmas, however, things did not go exactly as planned. Ben had invited Santa Clause to the morning service where he would hand out treats after the children's program.

Santa was actually Rick, a talented teenager who had played the role at different functions around town. Complete with costume, Rick arrived early and went to the balcony to put on his Santa outfit. The room was typically used for children's Sunday school but today the children would be involved in the worship service. Ben's family and I were the only ones who knew Santa was present.

During quiet moments, Rick tried to remain still in his hiding place since the fringe of his garment was laced with sleigh bells. In spite of his efforts, people would look around bewildered when they heard the muted sounds of bells.

Finally, after the children's program and my short sermon, Ben asked, "Now children, who in the world personifies the spirit of giving?"

I don't know if children understood those big words but someone from the congregation hollered, "Santa Clause!" At that moment, with bells ringing and pillows bouncing under a huge red coat, Rick came down the stairs with an enthusiastic, "Ho, Ho, Ho!"

Santa dragged the bag of oranges and candy to the front of the church and gave another hearty, "Ho, Ho, Ho!" He was having lots of fun. More fun than Miss Goodell thought decent folks should have in church. She sat, staring straight ahead. She would not look at Santa. He should have left her to herself, but he went to the pew on the outside aisle where she was seated. He leaned over and kissed her.

Isel waved her hand threateningly at him, then said clearly enough to be heard throughout the sanctuary, "I don't believe in you!" She never took her eyes off the wall in front of the church. Santa went to the back and passed out the candy to the true believers.

After a few days I stopped by to see Isel. She said that she was paralyzed with fear. She knew Santa wasn't real but her childhood would not allow her to relax. I prayed for her as she relived the wounds of her childhood and found new grace. She was gracious to Rick even though he was Santa.

⌖⌖

Thinking influences behavior. I tried different approaches to create new thought patterns. It is easy to develop tunnel vision, stare with the mind straight ahead, and only see what one wants to see, especially in spiritual practice.

Maybe one way to interrupt routine thought patterns was to rearrange the church furniture. Wouldn't it be nice to have a sanctuary that was wider than it was long? We ought to experiment to test if we like the seating arranged differently.

I talked my idea over with Ben. Saturday night we changed the furniture around in the sanctuary. The pulpit was next to the wall anyway so the choir was already off to the side of the pulpit. But now the pulpit was in front of a window on the side of the church sanctuary instead of the end. The pews were four deep in four rows which radiated out from the pulpit.

Anxiously, I waited the reaction of the saints as they entered the Lord's house.

"What on earth happened here?"

"This furniture is sacred and so is its arrangement, Pastor. "

I quickly replied, "It didn't cost us any money to see if we would like a building designed this way. "

"Oh, okay," I heard.

After a couple of Sundays, folks got used to the new arrangement and liked it. The only difficulty was those who usually sat on the back row. They talked during the sermon. Now they could be heard and it was distracting me. It was simpler to return the pews the way God meant them to be.

⊠⊠⊠

Ben said, "Pastor, we have a large group who just come for Sunday school and then leave. They don't stay for worship. Why don't we reverse the services this week during revival and not tell anyone?"

It was a challenge to get one lady and her large family to stay to hear the preaching. She would leave no matter how combined we tried to make Sunday school and worship. She was not going to stay. She had no husband to go home to. She didn't have to fix dinner for anyone at a fixed time. She just was not going to put up with two services at any one time.

Why not try having Church before Sunday school? The evangelist agreed when we told him all the good points of it. He could preach to as many as fifteen more people. That impresses most preachers. So without announcement, the next Sunday we had preaching first. Oh, it was going well. The people were attentive, and Ben and I were pleased that Elizabeth and her family were all getting to hear the gospel.

But the evangelist didn't know when to let go of a good thing. If one preaching service is good, a long one must be better, and he didn't quit when Sunday school should have been over. Elizabeth did. The sermon continued past the usual Sunday school hour. Elizabeth stood and summoned her large family from their scattered places in the sanctuary. When the grandchildren, their parents, and grandma had all gathered in the small foyer, they exited.

They got into several cars parked along the building. Elizabeth's car didn't have a muffler. She paused a little longer than usual next to the church building. With one foot on the accelerator and the other on the brake, she protested our plan of evangelism.

⊠⊠⊠

One spring day as I was at the college track, I met a man who was interested in attending our church. He and his family were new in the area. They were living in a motel until they located a house. Bob worked for Exxon's subsidiary, Monterey Coal Company. He was overseas for several years, but now employed in our town. He wanted to be in the states while his sons were in high school, and his daughter went to her first year of college.

Bob and his family became our friends. They were a big help to our church. We were thankful for the day they found a house. Because Marna had gone overseas with Bob, he wanted to buy her a big house. He did. It was a newer home in a newly developed section outside of town. To a pastor who was living in a Sears Roebuck catalogue parsonage, bought for a few thousand dollars, Bob and Marna's house seemed like a castle.

Bob and Marna were hospitable, practical people, and hosted church activities. In cold weather we had evening services in their living room. I especially remember a beautiful communion service on a New Year's Eve in their house. We felt close to God and each other as we sat facing the glowing fireplace. Bob's daughter was home from college and several other young people gathered to sing and pray and share what God was doing in their lives.

Bob's physical exercise created spiritual lessons for our congregation. I ran when I wanted to run, which was occasionally. I ran for fun. Bob ran every day. His new home was on a golf course next to a cemetery. Bob ran on the golf course and through the grave yard after they bought the house. I was not disciplined enough to go outside town and run with him consistently. Bob was a committed runner. Even on vacation, he would stop along the highway, turn the driving over to his family, and run. When in cities, he would run. His family was embarrassed, but proud of his determination. He was a member of the "One Hundred Day Club," which meant he had run for one hundred consecutive days.

One day Bob sprung a new idea on us. He planned to bicycle across the United States the next summer. It sounded too much for a fifty-five year old man to attempt. He'd had polio as a child. His face was partially drawn. In spite of our doubt, He trained and decided on a route. His boys drove to the west coast in a Volkswagen Beetle and they met him at the San Diego Airport.

He bicycled across America from San Diego to Portland, Maine. He had four weeks' vacation, but he could only be gone two weeks at a time. Since our town was halfway between the east and west coast, the schedule worked out fine.

His two boys, Kurt and Carl, pitched a tent each

night and carried an extra bike on top of the VW. Cactus needles punctured his tires. That was his only bicycle trouble but not his only challenge. The engine of the VW burned out trying to keep up with Bob across the desert of Arizona.

I asked Bob to take an evening service and tell what he had learned bicycling across the United States. We were inspired by the spirit of this courageous, determined man. He shared the lessons God had taught him.

"You don't deserve to coast down a hill until you have pedaled up."

"You never know what thirst is until you cross the desert in 108 degree heat."   "You can get sore in places you never even knew existed."

Bob explained at one point, when the VW quit, he was tempted to quit. He encountered a schoolteacher who was trying to do a similar feat. Bob thought he had to keep on going to encourage the young teacher. Together they helped each other. The lesson he found in meeting this stranger: "God is our ever present encourager. God looks like your neighbor."

"Lord," I prayed, "You guided and protected Bob over the deserts of our great West and over the rolling hills of our Midwest and the mountains of our East, I trust you to help me through the deserts and plains and mountains of being a pastor to people who will not change and will never have the faith to build a building. I'll be your knight here forever."

The love for the kingdom was alive and well.

CHAPTER SEVEN

SPIRITUAL AND PHYSICAL WORK

I have always considered myself pastor to any who had a need. Not just those in our church but to any who did not have a pastor. Often I would be at the bedside of someone whose family or neighbor attended church but the patient did not.

Ministering to all, regardless of creed or lack of creed, is a great area of outreach. If I could help them in their sickness, they would serve the King in their health. I always wanted to present myself and the church in a way which would not diminish Christ.

I visited a church I served twenty-eight years before. A lady in her eighties leaned over to me as we watched her grandchildren on the platform. She said to me that on a specific date over twenty years before, "At five in the morning you were the most important man to me in the whole world." I remembered praying with her as she prepared to undergo major surgery. She, at that time, was not attending church but God's grace moved in her heart because a pastor stood near.

St. Louis was sixty miles to the south, and anyone with a serious illness went to one of several hospitals there for treatment. The father-in-law of one of the young ladies who attended our church was scheduled for throat cancer surgery. They had no pastor and she asked me to be present during the operation. I left home early to be in St. Louis by six AM.

I glanced out the window as I departed the elevator on the eleventh floor. There was a generous view of the city with the 'Gateway to the West Arch' off to the east. I was in a hurry to get to the patient's room before he was taken to surgery, so did not stop to look at the view. I made a mental note to enjoy the view some time that day.

I found the patient's room and the daughter-in-law introduced me to the family. The man's wife was attractively dressed, and I noticed her bright red shoes. I wondered why she was so dressed up for a surgery. After I prayed with the family, I visited with them for a few minutes. Two men with "transporter" on their name tags arrived. They loaded him on a gurney, and took him to surgery. I went with the family, which included seven or eight people, to the surgical waiting area.

I joked with the family that I hoped the transporters of their loved one would be received by agreeable lifters. My neighbor had been admitted to the same hospital and had suffered humiliation. I told them the story.

The hospital staff was unionized. One day my

neighbor was to be taken from his room down to x-ray. He had a tumor removed from the ankle and required bone graft. The doctor wanted to check if the bone was growing. The pushers took him to x-ray after the nurses had loaded him onto the cart. The lifters were gone on coffee break, and he waited for some time, until they returned and put him on the x-ray table. He had the x-rays, and was put back on a gurney, but not the right one. The pushers would not put him on the right table. The lifters had left. The staff had a union discussion. Two hours later, the proper lifters returned, and then the pushers could not be found. Another hour passed. When the pushers were found, they never delivered a more irate patient to his room.

The family laughed and relaxed, and I sank back in an overstuffed chair, and listened to them talk through their concern. The patient smoked for thirty-five years. He was only fifty. The surgeon said he might have to take the voice box. They assured each other that would not happen. I grimaced within. I knew the operating team would do what they had to do to save his life. I remained silent. An hour later I rose to seek out a restroom.

I left the surgery waiting room, turned right, and saw a classroom at the end of the hall with a window. It had been occupied by student nurses hearing a lecture earlier. I thought of my promise to view the city from the hospital and walked to the classroom. I passed the restrooms on the way. The men's restroom was the first one I came to. I said to myself, "I'll view the city first from the classroom, and then use the restroom." I didn't know if the room would be used again soon, and I didn't want to lose the opportunity.

The view was spectacular. The sun was reflecting off the top of the Gateway Arch. The river had a layer of fog just above it making it easy to trace the meandering river between Missouri and Illinois. The tug boats were pushing extended loads. Tom Sawyer must have had many days just like this. I day dreamed for a while. I wished Cindy could enjoy this view. The problems of the church and finances seemed remote. I even forgot the family waiting to hear news of their beloved father.

After a few minutes of enjoying the scene, I went back down the hall and into the first rest room. No urinals. That's strange, but not uncommon. I had been in rest rooms without urinals. I went into the first stall. A sanitary napkin dispenser was attached to the restroom stall. Now this is different. And just as I determined I was in the wrong rest room, I heard the sound of high heeled shoes coming down the hall.

An individual would be walking this direction for only one of two reasons, and I was sure it was not to look at the river out the class room window. The family was not interested in going to look at scenery with their thoughts on the patient. I went into the second stall and locked the door. I sat on the toilet and picked up my feet. I hoped there was only one person coming.

When I saw red shoes in the next stall, bright red shoes, I quickly got off my perch, and keeping my feet out of view of the first stall, I made my exit. What did she think? Did she see me? Did she think I was some kind of weirdo? If she saw me, would she tell the family? I wished I could die. But I went back to the surgery waiting area as calmly as I could and buried my face in a magazine. I was followed shortly by red shoes. Their owner continued to look as if nothing strange had happened and her only concern was her husband.

After the extensive surgery, the doctor told her and the children that he was sorry but the voice box had to be removed. He thought they had been able to get all the cancer. The wife looked at me and screamed, "Where is God? My husband never did anything to deserve this!" And then she sobbed for several minutes, hurting for her loss, and that of her husband.

I had no answers. None was expected. It was the cry of desperation and lament. Every loss needs a proper grief response. Unfortunately, she and her three adult children each continued to reach for cigarettes as they had all morning.

***

Sometimes actions and their effect are easy to see, or at least that is what we think. Often there is no apparent answer to why bad things happen. My first funeral was a grave side service for a newborn. It was the second loss for the young couple. Their baby had spinal meningitis and lived only six days. The doctor told them to burn the clothing, the blankets, and destroy all the utensils the baby had used.

I went home and watched my son play. I recalled all the hope and aspirations and dreams we had for him.

All the fun and anticipation waiting for him to be born reminded me to be grateful. I tried to feel the couple's hurt, not once but twice, as they laid the expressions of their love in the ground.

The community was not so tender. The couple was from the wrong side of the tracks. He was Native American. They were poor, and had little. I heard, "He carries the disease."

"He's no good."

"They ought to get out of town before our children get sick too."

I prayed, "Lord, help me to show these people how to love."

※※※

I was frustrated by people's cruelty. I saw it as a spiritual problem. When I am frustrated by the spiritual, I have been able to find relief in the physical. It made me feel like I was accomplishing something for the King.

When we first came to try out as a ministry couple, we were shown the parsonage in the dark. We later knew why. The plaster was cracking. The wall paper in the bath room was peeling. There were large bare spots on the lap siding, and most of the paint was curled and flaking.

I told the church board we ought to paint. "We know that pastor, but we can't afford the paint."

The hardware store was having a sale. "Buy one, get one free." Everybody wanted to buy the free gallon. But they got serious, and four families volunteered to buy a gallon of paint. I bought one, so that made ten gallons with our free ones. I figured it would take twelve, but we had a good start.

I started scraping but I hate to scrape. I didn't mind painting the exterior, but why did I have to scrape? But daily I scraped.

I wasn't about to let this house continue to be an eyesore. The other houses in our neighborhood had aluminum siding or brick veneer. It wasn't in my job description, and I had little help, but Cindy and I scraped the two story house. The neighbors spoke proudly of us. They had given up hope of it ever being painted. They thanked us for our work on the church owned house.

One day I was painting the back side of the house. Standing on a ladder, I could see down the street, and two people were making house calls. They were across the street and headed our way. Various neighbors slammed their doors or refused to answer. They were from a cult and had a reputation for being hard to get rid of, if given an opening. Most of our neighbors didn't start a conversation with these people, if they could avoid it.

I stayed out of sight, and waited to see what would happen at our house. My sister, a nurse at the Cleveland Clinic, was visiting us. We tried to convince Betty to get a job at Carlinville Hospital and live with us. The church needed her tithe and another young adult was always appreciated. Maybe we could find her a boy friend.

The two cult members knocked at the door, and Betty answered. "Could they come in and talk about God?"

"This is a parsonage," my sister responded, "We already got God."

That did not deter the visitors. They continued to press to enter. Betty was active in her church and had taken college Bible courses. After a time of talking to the visitors, she decided she needed some help. She called back into the house, "Cindy, these people want to talk to you."

Together, they talked on and on. Cindy was too polite to send them away, but was not going to let them inside. I was painting around the corner and could hear the conversation. Every once in a while Cindy would ask, "Where's Blair? I just don't know what happened to him. I wish my husband was here to talk to you."

After several minutes, the baby cried. Cindy and Betty excused themselves to care for the baby. They shut the door, not a slam but firmly, and our visitors went to the next house. I came in for lunch, and as we ate, they gave me all the details. They had some visitors and couldn't get rid of them.

"Where were you?" They asked.

I answered with, "I bet you said 'where is Blair. I just don't know what happened to him. I wish he were here." And then I burst into laughter, and two women were very upset. I quickly found I liked to paint. Painting wasn't so bad after all compared to an angry wife and sister.

⌘

While I felt I could work on the exterior of the house, I had no confidence to tackle anything major inside. I was thrilled to learn Cindy's parents were coming for a couple of weeks. Cindy's dad, a carpenter, textured the ceiling and concealed the cracks in the plaster. It was tedious and required a skilled touch. If he pushed too hard, the loose plaster would fall on his head when he withdrew the brush.

We ordered wall paper from Dad's supplier in Omaha. It came by bus a couple days before Cindy's parents were to return home.. He wall papered the living room and dining room in one day. With the new drapes Cindy had bought through the J C Penny catalogue, the rooms were elegant. All the drapes had to be special ordered because the ceilings were ten feet high, and the windows extended from a few inches above the floor, to within a few inches of the ceiling.

Cindy's father rebuilt the back steps. Also he gave me some ideas on remodeling the bathroom so we could add a shower. Over several months, the house really was transformed. The porch extended across the front and half way around the side of the house. It was painted white with green trim. The porch deck was uneven but we put outdoor carpet on it. We were very pleased with the way things looked. It now belonged in the neighborhood. People commented on how nice it looked.

In fact, they commented too much. "We must be paying the pastor too much. Since the parsonage looks so nice and that is part of his pay, we should decrease the salary." That talk was limited to one family. They didn't comment on the fact that Cindy and I had painted. Cindy's dad had done the interior work. I had paid for the material.

Leo and I built shelves for my office. My wife sacrificed

to buy the expensive drapes for the high windows throughout the house.

I prayed, "Lord, help me to love these people like you do."

"Oh, I see Lord; you're ashamed of them too."

"We'll love them together." Physical work was spiritual work too.

Chapter Eight

AND THE TWO BECAME FOUR

"*He has committed to us the message of reconciliation.*" II Corinthians 5:19

The professor's words rang through my mind, "Reconciliation! That is our business. That is our reason for being." I was a long way from a seminary classroom. The reconciliation for which I existed seemed to be far from the minds of people. As a young pastor my greatest heartache was to see parents and their teens disagree and pull apart.

My parents and I had a good relationship. I didn't understand why other kids had struggles with their parents. If I didn't agree with mom and dad, I didn't disobey, I sulked. Even as an immature teen I prayed for my parents and our disagreements. I knew the Bible promised that I would benefit by honoring them. I would benefit if they made good decisions. I would benefit if they directed me to the best instead of the better. They trained me in the way I should go.

Of course, I didn't always think my parents were right. In my mind I thought my way was the right. Sometimes they agreed with me. More often I just prayed with no results, or at least it seemed like it. But after it was all done, mom and dad were still my parents, and we were not enemies.

Not so with the couple who sat in the parsonage living room. They had come to be married. I could see fear in their eyes. They started by asking, "Do ministers have to say that part in the ceremony about, 'If anyone has any reason why this couple should not be married, let them speak now or forever hold their peace?'" I assured them I did not have to ask the question, but asked why they wanted it omitted. "Is someone against you being married?" I enquired. That was what opened a flood of confession as they told their story.

When Jane was fourteen and Larry was seventeen, they ran away. Jane had become pregnant, but the baby had died before birth. They were gone about a year, living in different places in the West. They decided to come home and face the consequences.

Both sets of parents had been against them dating. Jane was too young. Larry didn't have a skill. Jane's parents drew a line for Larry. "Either you join the service and get out of our lives, or we will have you arrested." Larry joined the military. Jane was sent to a school for girls about eighty miles away. It was a school with harsh discipline and rigid rules. Over the years, after the forced break up, Jane and Larry dated others but their distance did not keep them from writing to each other.

As they sat before me, Jane was now twenty one and Larry was twenty four. He was working for a car manufacturer near St. Louis, a good job with good pay. They had been living together for three years. They wanted to be married, and since Jane had attended our church when she was young, she wanted to be married in the church.

"Why did you wait until now to get married?" I asked.

Jane said she wanted to be old enough that her parents could not stop them from getting married.

"Are you pregnant now?" I asked.

"No," she responded, and neither of them seemed shocked that I asked. I guess if a couple has been living together, it is no big thing if the preacher asks if you are pregnant.

We spent time together in premarital counseling. I was talking to a couple who had lived together for three years and had loved each other for seven. They had been struggling against pressure on their marriage longer than my wife and I had been married. I wanted to help them more than just legalize their relationship.

"Are you inviting your parents to the wedding?" I asked.

They both responded firmly, "No."

"Oh Lord," I prayed silently, "help them to heal."

I explained they should invite both sets of parents to their ceremony. "Tell them you are old enough to be legally married and would like their blessing. If there is any lingering resentment, let it not be on your part. Put the decision whether to attend the ceremony in your parents' court." I assured them I would not give an opportunity to protest the marriage during the ceremony.

The evening of the rehearsal, Jane's mother still did not know they were getting married. The wedding was the next day. Taking the young woman aside, I quietly told her, "forever is a long time to be estranged from one's mother." I did everything but threaten not to marry them if the mother was not at least invited.

The next afternoon, a nervous bride and groom waited for their guests. At the announced starting time, not a minute earlier, both sets of parents came in. I recognized the mother. She worked at the hospital as a nurse. I had not connected the two, but now more than ever, I wanted healing in their relationship. I wanted it for them. I wondered about the bitterness which had developed. How deep were the scars? Could I make a difference for this family?

"Oh, God, please help them put the strife behind them. Give them a new start." Now I knew the two who should become one again, and it wasn't the bride and groom. The prayer was the deep sigh of my heart.

"Dearly beloved...." There was no giving the bride away. The audience just stared ahead. The sisters and brothers of the groom were afraid to show joy, because they didn't know how the moms would receive it. When the vows were exchanged there was no doubt in my mind that the bride and groom meant it to be forever. They had already overcome so much. Both were attractive. They were not overcoming poverty. Larry had a good job.

Yes, any normal mother would have been against a thirteen year old dating. It wasn't a mother's dream for her under aged daughter to elope with a boy that had no visible means of supporting her. But that was in the past. This couple had overcome the scars of continual put downs, "you're not worthy" trash talk for eight years.

A little piece of life had become a wedge forcing a chasm between mother and daughter. Larry's family thought the bride's mother hated him. His parents had raised a good boy, now a man, but Jane's mother was clinging to a disagreement eight years old.

I prayed for them aloud as a couple. I prayed for their health and future children. I asked God to bring healing to their relationships. I asked God to bless their home with a supporting family. In my nervousness about the reaction of the parents, I prayed longer than normal, and finally pronounced, "You are now husband and wife."

Then, I said, "You may kiss the bride." That's when something beautiful happened. Everybody wanted to kiss. His parents hugged the bride and welcomed her into their family. Her mother cried like a true mother at a wedding. She said she was sorry. She welcomed the groom into her home as her son.

The mother humbly stood before the bride and groom and said from the depth of a mother's heart that cared for her daughter, "Thank you, thank you, for inviting me to the wedding. I wish you had given me time to get my hair fixed." And they all laughed.

In time, I saw the mother and daughter shopping together. And whenever I saw them, I knew God had used me to fulfill my purpose of reconciler.

Not all reconciliation attempts worked.

One evening Cindy and I took our youth roller skating. It was a joint activity with several other Churches of the Nazarene. I was tired and glad to be getting away from the activity by 9:00 P.M. This would get us home a little after 10. I asked one family, riding with us, what time their father went to bed. He had been disagreeable with the kids and didn't allow much freedom. I was glad he had given them permission to go with us roller skating. I wanted to stay on his good side for their sake.

To my question of the time dad goes to bed, they responded, "Dad goes to bed after the news."

"Oh good," I responded, "You will get home before he goes to bed." In that time zone the news is from 10 to 10:30 P.M.

"No," one of the siblings said, "we mean Dad goes to bed after the 5 o'clock news."

Some people are not reconcilable by their own choice. Their wounds are deep and they don't want to face the emotional pain that will allow healing. The father did not have the will to bend. He insisted everything go his way. Finally he broke. His rigidity was the direct opposite of his kid's spontaneity. He left his beautiful wife and five children. He lived alone, until he died of a heart condition, because he could not adjust to anybody else's way of doing things. Even the innocent things they did every day grated on him.

I heard one of our church families was having trouble. They had been in trouble a long time, but they didn't know it. Since I was the pastor, I took it upon myself to help them. The couple had ten children all under twelve. All of them were born at home without a doctor. The children regularly attended church, and the mother came occasionally. The father never attended, and worked even less. It was rumored to him that the neighbor man had been in the couple's house doing something immoral. Certain men in town liked others to think they could seduce another man's wife. They told elaborate tales that were lies, most of the time.

I was told where I could find the father of the ten children so I went to the house. I told him his wife and kids needed him. I wasn't sure why they needed him, since all he did was consume the drink he bought with the welfare check.

"If I go home to my wife, that will condone her adultery," he told me.

So I asked. "Are you sure she committed adultery?"

"The man told me himself, he did it," he said.

I knew the other man. He was as lazy as this one. "Do you believe him?" I asked.

"Sure I do. And I told him I had been with his wife too," he spouted in response.

This was getting interesting. Perhaps it was some licentious desire in my heart that made me ask, "Did you sleep with his wife?"

"Nope, but he doesn't know that, and if I go back to

my wife, he will think I didn't believe him, and then he won't believe me." How could a man so lazy come up with such complicated reasoning?

"Besides," he continued, "he doesn't know that I have been going home after dark every night. We are going to have another baby."

It was often hard to know who was speaking. Was it a wounded man? Was it someone who wanted to change? Or, was it a man who wanted to impress others?

⊠⊠⊠

I tried to help people be genuine. I preached a sermon about being an open Christian, "known and read by all men." I encouraged them to be vulnerable, to let people see you, the real you.

I closed my sermon with an illustration from the life of Alexander the Great. A young man was brought to him who had fled during battle.

"What is your name?" enquired the ruler. When there was no answer to his question, the leader repeated the question louder. "What is your name?" According to the story, the young soldier said, "My name is Alexander."

Alexander the Great replied, "Either change your name or change your character."

As I was telling the story, I put great emphasis and asked forcefully, "What is your name?" When I asked the question a second time, my two year old son, sitting with the nursery attendant on the back row boomed as loud as he could, "Boyd Russell Rorabaugh."

The illustration never carried the punch I thought it would after the congregation quit rolling with laughter. Boyd stole the show but even laughter is reconciling and good for the heart.

CHAPTER NINE

THE PASTOR GETS BAPTIZED

My grandfather was a dairy farmer in central Pennsylvania. Dairy farming is a difficult life because milking must be done morning and evening seven days a week. My grandparents had been married over fifty years. I had never known of them to leave the farm except for part of a day. I asked him if he and my grandmother had ever eaten at a restaurant.

Grandfather thought for a moment. He recalled only one time they had eaten at a restaurant. It was their first wedding anniversary, and he wanted to treat "Mom" to a meal out. He hitched the horses to the buggy, and took his young wife to La Jose where there was a restaurant on the first floor and a hotel over it.

After they had eaten, Grandfather was feeling proud to have taken Grandma out to eat. But according to Grandfather, Grandma thought differently. "Mom said, 'I can cook better than this', and we never went out again."

Perhaps that is where I get my "eat at home" disposition. I grew up in a small village with no restaurants nearby. I never remember eating at a restaurant with my family, but did when the church youth group went to conventions.

My wife grew up in Omaha, Nebraska. Eating out was their Sunday custom. Her family often went to the Blackstone Hotel, famous for its steaks.

After Cindy and I got married, I struggled to justify spending money to eat out.

During the seminary years, we tried to eat out one evening a week. We had moved from a large community, Kansas City, with all the wonderful places to eat. Now we were in a small town with nothing. At least that is what I tried to tell my wife. We would have to be satisfied eating at home. There just were no places to eat out in this town. Besides, we didn't have money for restaurants.

Somehow, Cindy found there was at least one place that cooked chicken. Since it was located next to the high school, it was a hangout for the youth to buy snacks. We had to try it. The chicken was a combination of deep fried and pressure cooked. They cooked the potatoes with the chicken. The food wasn't bad, and any lack of variety in the food was made up for by the attention our baby received.

The owner and his wife were in their fifties and evidently teenagers were their only customers. So when we came in, they came out from behind the counter and the kitchen to take turns holding our little one.

We never had to struggle with our infant son, Boyd, while we ate. The owners were glad to have customers besides teens. They made sure the baby didn't bother us while we ate. They held him the whole time. The owner had a large ring of keys which he took from his belt and gave to Boyd to play and teeth on. I guess we never thought about germs, just about what entertained the baby.

We had heard of another restaurant located on the town square. When we asked about Dresdon's we were told, "No one goes there but old people."

I looked for other possibilities since my wife was going into restaurant depravation. Besides, I wanted a different menu than fried chicken. The restaurant on the square had no fried food. They offered only meals, no snack foods. The wallpaper looked a hundred years old. Abraham Lincoln had once slept in Carlinville, and he may have seen that wall paper. Some of the clientele probably could have told about Lincoln's visit if they remembered their parents' stories.

When we stepped into Dresdon's, the youngest people we saw were the owners. Like the combination snack and chicken restaurant, these owners were also in their fifties. Every other person, and the restaurant was nearly full, would never see their sixties again.

But people are people, and these customers watched as we walked to the table. They probably had little contact with young people and were glad to see a couple with a baby. They also wanted to hold Boyd. We felt at home from the very first meal at Dresdon's. The owners were friendly and the meals were economical. It was difficult to fix a comparable meal at home for the cost.

One evening we took Miss Goodell out to eat at Dresden's. It was like old home day, like a homecoming festival. She had been confined to the two blocks between church and her home for a long time and hadn't seen her many friends.

The town was divided along generation lines. There was the greasy spoon and the old age home restaurant. The majority of people never had been in both. They fit in either one or the other. For those who found the courage to develop friends on both ends of the spectrum, it was very rewarding. In one, the teens were fun. The food was good. The noise was terrible. In the other, the food was home cooked and healthy. The silence gave way to friendly chatter, and Cindy found that small towns weren't all that lonely.

The older people were not that much different than the young people. People of all ages have relationship problems. The teens had their spats and attitudes could be seen in their grandparents.

Mr. Eller, a man in his late seventies, attended church for the past twenty five years. When he was younger, in his sixties, he walked, but now he was dependent on a ride. I regularly gave Mr. Eller a ride to church. He lived about five blocks from the church, so it was easy to stop along the way at Miss Goodell's, and drive them both to church in one trip. I had been giving both of them rides most of the winter.

One day, as I walked Isel to her door, she asked

me to come and see her the next day. If something was bothering Miss Goodell, Isel was the kind of individual who preferred to speak out and get it off her mind.

"Pastor," she began, "I am not going to ride to church with you anymore."

"What is the trouble?" I asked. I expected to hear about God giving her one good leg and she should be using it.

"It's that Mr. Eller. The whole way to and from church I know what is on his mind, "she explained. It is only two blocks, I thought, but didn't comment.

"Oh? What is on his mind, Miss Goodell?" I tried to not show any expression because I knew this was going to be good.

"Well, I can't tell you because you're a man, but he looks at me with more interest than he should."

"Has he ever said anything to you?" I asked.

"No, but he doesn't need to. I know what is on his mind. From now on Jerry Strode can pick me up. If Jerry can't, and if I can't walk, I won't be there, because I will not ride in a car with Mr. Eller. It just isn't proper."

And that settled that. She would not ride in the same car with him again, although she had always sat in the front and he in the back. He always said to me as I picked him up first, "I will get in the back, because I know it is easier for Isel to get in the front with her brace."

The trouble was not Mr. Eller. He was always a gentlemen and a fine friend. But even a lady in her older years who never married can have thoughts of love and it bothered her to have those feelings.

⊠⊠⊠

Two sisters, ages fourteen and fifteen, who attended our church lacked Miss Goodell's inhibitions. The whole family had problems with mental capacity but these two girls had particularly empty shelves. They were boy crazy. Conversations with these girls were always about boyfriends. They talked about the dates they were going to have, and about being engaged. They were only fourteen and fifteen.

I asked their mother if they really were engaged. Her response was, "I don't know." She knew there were some boys that hung around their house. She didn't think anything was going on.

It turned out her shelf was as empty as and a lot shorter than her two daughters. Both daughters had babies, and both girls insisted they could keep the babies and live on welfare with their mother. "Lord, how can this be happening in my church?" I felt the guilt of failure. The two girls never felt guilty.

⊠⊠⊠

The joy of bringing reconciliation to a family and restoring them to the church compensated for the difficulties. I felt like a doctor must feel treating a patient who is not sure he is sick. The sister of a man told me her brother was having problems in his marriage. I was not sure he realized his marriage was in jeopardy.

His sister asked me, "Please go and visit them," On the first visit, no mention of trouble was made. People don't usually admit to problems before the preacher, since they want to look good. I had not met them before, so they were less than candid. Later, I heard that she kicked him out, so I went back. This time she was honest about the marital problem.

"Yes," she said. "We are splitting up for good this time. I kicked him out."

"What's the problem?" I asked.

"He's been drinking. I'm sure he has been unfaithful to me. I see him with another woman frequently."

Adultery is terrible and leaves scars. I assured the broken wife that God cared. She had every right for a divorce. If she chose divorce, we would help her through the stress.

"Ginger, there is an option to separation or divorce. There is the path of forgiveness and reestablishing trust. If you love your husband and want to work on your marriage, God will help you, and I will give prayerful support."

Ginger and Ray had five children. Four were still at home; the youngest was five years old. I met with them as a couple. He never admitted to us that he was having an affair and I never mentioned it.

Ginger offered forgiveness in spite of the wrongs done to her. "You can come home if you will be faithful to me."

Ray said nothing. He gave no response. His silence left me thinking I had failed. I felt the husband would not change. They went to separate homes.

Sunday morning they came to church in separate cars,

and sat together with their four children, who still lived at home. When I gave the invitation to receive Christ's forgiveness, they all knelt at the altar. He poured out his heart through tears and sobs of grief. When he had finished praying, his face shone as one who had touched God and been forgiven.

We didn't have a baptistery in our church, but used the one at a nearby church. I arranged for the baptistery to be filled with water the next Sunday afternoon.

When we gathered at the church for baptism, the pastor apologized. The heater had been left on all night. The water was hot. He had been adding cold water, but it was still quite warm.

The whole family was going to be baptized. The father started the service by testifying to those who attended how God had saved his home. He appreciated the church introducing to him a new life. He thanked God for saving him from his sins. That was the most reserved Ray ever spoke.

Prior to baptizing them, I explained about the water, it was uncomfortably hot, but was safe. They all nodded they understood, but the eyes of the five year showed fear. I told her it was okay.

I slowly got into the water. It was uncomfortably warm. I had baptized in some very cold water and thought I preferred warm to cold but not hot.

I baptized Ray and then Ginger and the three older children. Everything was going well in spite of the hot water. The five year old tentatively put her foot into the two inches of water on the first step. Feeling the hot water, she jumped into the air and threw her legs around me. With one leg on either side of my shoulders, she wrapped her arms in a death grip around my head. She was completely out of the water and had no intentions of letting go, so I could baptize her with any dignity.

All that good theology I had shared with the family about baptism now had no meaning to her. The water was hot and she intended to stay out of it.

People watched from the front pews of the church. They knew the water was hot, because the little girl kept repeating, "The water is hot! The water is hot! The water is hot!" Each time she repeated "the water is hot", her voice grew higher in pitch and louder in volume. I tried to get her to both calm down, and to come down off my head, but she kept saying, "The water is hot!"

She didn't realize what a privilege it is to be baptized in hot water. Finally I decided the best thing was to just go under with her, so "In the same of the Father, Son, and Holy Spirit," I baptized myself and the little girl.

The King must have been proud of his knight who would sacrifice appearance for "one of these little ones."

Chapter Ten

THE LAYING ON OF HANDS

Not only was I a young pastor, I was also naive. I had grown up sheltered by a loving family and a community that took responsibility for every child in the village. My parents were active in the local church and were service oriented. Every child was known by the neighbors, and it was not easy to get away with pranks.

On the way home from school as a third grader, I threw stones at a purple martin bird house. The next door neighbor saw me and called the school. It was off school property, but I was in trouble at school. The same neighbors who reported misbehavior also supported our fund raisers and bought our never ending supply of garden seeds in the spring, assorted greeting cards, or homemade cookies, and loop potholders. To me, the world was a safe place.

I asked Jesus into my heart when I was in seventh grade. He freed me from the guilt of my committed sins. Since I did not use drugs, tobacco or alcohol, addictions were not my problem. My sins before Christ were usually of the spirit, not the flesh.

I was active in high school sports, summer baseball, church camps, and many church centered activities. My experiences were always good. My heroes were church youth workers, Sunday school and public school teachers, and sports coaches. I just believed at that time in my life everyone in church was trustworthy.

When I attended seminary, there were no courses on conflict and people skills. "Preach the Word of God and love the people and you will be okay." I guess they forgot Jesus said we were sheep going out among wolves.

One result of this wonderful innocent life is trust. I trusted adults in the church, and especially those who served on the church board because I expected them to have higher standards. I started my ministry with a mindset that people who are in church love the Lord and can be trusted. I was proud of my people and spoke well of them.

Reconciling and reactivating people who used to attend church was my priority. When I knocked on the doors of previous attendees, I was always greeted warmly. Usually they invited me into their homes and offered me something to eat or coffee to drink. We would talk about the weather or the crops. They would share about their children and then ask about my family. Sometimes I would ask them to worship again with us, but my usual practice was just to be there and let them talk.

Eventually the conversation would be about people they knew who attended the church. One family invariably was asked about. "Do the Hickenbockens still come to the church?"

"Oh yes," I would reply. "They serve on the board and Mrs. Hickenbocken calls on the sick. Aren't they wonderful people?"

I would receive a nod and husband and wife would look at each other. As I departed, I would think how good it is to have a church with good people.

One evening a young farmer who attended church with his wife and two little children, came to see me. He was new to our church and had recently been elected to the church board. As soon as he walked in the door I could tell something was wrong.

"Pastor," he said, "I don't know how to address this, so I will just tell you. I am going to kill someone. Hickenbocken makes a fuss over our baby when my wife is holding him. He asks if he can hold the baby. When he takes the baby he pinches my wife's breast."

The first time his wife had not said anything, thinking it was an accident, but it happened again so she told her husband. I assured the upset husband I would deal with the problem short of murder.

Wow! What should I do? I asked another mother with a young infant about it. She acknowledged it had been done to her. But more information was added. She and her family had been invited to the Hickenbocken's house for dinner. Mr. Hickenbocken was seated at the end of the dining room table. She was seated next to him. He rubbed his foot along her leg. She set her glass down hard and looked him in the eye, but did not say anything. She didn't tell her husband until much later.

I was in a conspiracy of silence. No one wanted to tell me, the innocent preacher. No one wanted to destroy the image of holiness he had in his mind of his people. Mostly, no one wanted to confront sin or the sinner.

I had promised the upset husband that I would deal with the problem. After all I was the knight on the King's business, and I was called to handle such things. Conversations with past church attendees came to mind. My words echoed like a curse inside me.

"Oh yes, aren't the Hickenbockens wonderful people." It caused me to remember I had been told, when college groups come, "we never send girls to the Hickenbockens." At the time I thought nothing of it, but figured they found girls too much trouble.

I had watched Mr. Hickenbocken as he sat on the end of his pew. He would lean over into the side aisle so he could see the young lady at the piano. He viewed the miniskirt or what it didn't cover as she shuffled on and off the piano bench. He stared as in a trance.

After hearing the accusation from the farmer, and the confirmation from another mother, I wrestled with the situation. I reasoned about how I could avoid confrontation. I struggled with myself. Why didn't I let him get murdered? Such unholy thoughts troubled me as I struggled within over what approach to take. There was no way but to face it. I prayed about it and went to see Hickenbocken.

He served as a trustee on the church board. I told him that because of his behavior — and I explicitly said — his continual practice of touching the breast of mothers when taking their babies, he would not be allowed to serve on the board beyond the present church year, which was ending in two months. He never denied laying hands on the women. He just smiled as if innocent of all wrong.

A couple of days after my message to Mr. Hickenbocken, there was a resignation letter on the pulpit. Both Mr. and Mrs. Hickenbocken resigned from their church positions. I told the church board what had happened and what I had done. One response was, "Oh, Pastor, he has been doing that for years." Some knew of this behavior and had not told me. They were afraid of losing one family but instead had lost several families. God and the church had been betrayed.

One of the board members said, "If an older pastor had told them, they might have stayed with the church." Yes, I was young and immature in many ways, but I was not going to be party to covering someone's sin. It cast a blemish on our church. It also brought a change to my life. It ruined by idealistic image that I had of my lay people. I know people have problems, but problems are not sin. My naivety was gone.

The Hickenbockens were only in church one more time while I was pastor. Their last time in church was the pastoral vote. They cast their vote and left the worship service. When the ballots were counted there were two "No" votes against me as pastor. All other votes were "Yes".

Should I have done it differently? Should I have called my district superintendent who was ill? Should I have called the church board together and asked for advice?

Those who knew the offense were enablers. By their inaction they were silently assenting and watching while family after family left because of his gift of "laying on of hands." Some didn't know of the problem until the board meeting, and they were proud of their pastor standing for right. However, one protested, "The Hickenbockens were going to give a thousand dollars in the building program."

In a later congregation, I faced a similar situation. I called the district leadership. I talked to the church board, but in the end I was the one who faced the anger. I exposed the immorality of a leader that a few knew about and ignored. Young or old, new or experienced as pastor, I have one heart and mind. I will be faithful to my King. If I am considered a success or failure by others it is secondary to hearing my King say, "Well done good and faithful servant." The words of Job 6:10 have comforted me when I stand on moral issues. "This gives me comfort despite all the pain--that I have not denied the words of the holy God." (Living Bible)

Dealing with embarrassing issues was different with another couple in a later congregation. One mid-afternoon as I walked by their home I saw Jim and Sally on the porch. I greeted them. We talked about the weather and their new jobs. They had both been out of work for some time and were thankful for their jobs. Suddenly it came to me; it is the middle of the afternoon. "Is your work day over," I asked.

They looked at each other, and without a word between them, agreed to tell what happened. She said, "No, we both were called to the school this afternoon. Sarah is on the couch in the house instead of at school. She is in time out forever." I asked what happened. Naïve preachers tread where angels fear to trod. Besides, she is only in first grade, what could she do that was bad enough to get suspended for the day.

The mother said, "She was touching the flowers." It was December. There were no flowers to touch. I didn't know the term. When she realized I didn't know what she meant, she expanded so I would know, "Flowers is the term for 'private parts." Sarah was asked by a little boy in the school dining room if she wanted to touch his flower and she was caught by a teacher's aide.

This couple did not enter the conspiracy of silence. They thanked the teacher for telling them. They instructed their first grader not to touch the flowers. We laughed together and agreed it was childhood innocence and a learning experience for the parents and the preacher. I'll certainly be careful about how I refer to flowers.

Although sexual sin gets the attention, financial misconduct is more common. One way is to use money inappropriately to buy influence, or more subtlety, to make one feel good. When we first arrived at our church, I was told that one of our members, who attended without her husband, had purchased a new car for the previous pastor. That sounded wonderful. The Lincoln God had given us was twelve years old and no longer reliable. It was a temptation to let it known that we needed a car.

Of course, it was obvious that our car was well used. We didn't say anything because we had determined that God would make the arrangements and supply our needs. One day the woman who had given a new car to the previous pastor, came to the house. "Pastor," she said, "I want to purchase a new piano for your home. Cindy needs a new piano to teach her lessons." We had purchased an old upright piano from a moving neighbor and it was getting plenty of use.

Something didn't seem right. My spirit was not at peace, so I replied, "Thank you for your generosity, but God is taking good care of us. If you will faithfully pay your tithe, we will be well cared for." She insisted she was paying her tithes, then went her way offended by my refusal to accept her gift.

Some times you wish you could take your words back. A new piano would have been wonderful. Cindy worked hard; she deserved it.

Was I being proud?

Was not wanting to accept such a generous gift being presumptuous?

Was God meeting a need and I was not cooperating?

That evening I went to bed with those questions but satisfied that I had done the right thing. I hoped it was for the right reason.

A few days later I was at the community pastors' association meeting. We were a close group, isolated from, and rarely able to have fellowship among pastors of our own denominations. We shared concerns from our lives, families, and churches before we prayed at the meetings.

One of the pastors said he had a major problem in his church. He was concerned for one of his men, a building contractor facing bankruptcy. The builder had done some work for the church for several thousand dollars. The church had mailed the payment and thought all was taken care of. The builder approached the pastor about six weeks after the money had been sent and asked why he had not been paid.

The pastor looked into the situation and found the treasurer had made full payment several weeks before. The check had been cashed by the contractor's wife but she had not told her husband. The man's wife was the member of my church who was giving expensive gifts to pastors. She had been giving expensive gifts to others for several months without her husband's knowledge.

I was a very contrite man as I walked home from our meeting. On my own, without the check of the Spirit, I would have accepted the piano. She wanted to feel good. She wanted to bless her pastor but the money was not hers to give.

It reminded me of King David who was offered free land for the temple along with the sacrificial animal and wood for the fire. David said "I will not give to the Lord that which costs me nothing." A review of the giving records showed she had not given the church any substantial amounts of money, which I would have returned to the family.

"Lord," I prayed, "thank you for keeping me from further hurting that man. Help them to resolve their problems." Since I do not know what is in the heart of others, I depend on God who knows all.

CHAPTER ELEVEN

THE LOST IS RESTORED

Loss is a part of life. Some losses are recoverable, like health that is restored through proper diet or medical attention, and sometimes the unexplained miracles. Some loses seem big at the time, but prove to be inconsequential in the larger picture. At times it is the pastor who is restored.

We received a frantic call one day from Marna. Her husband, Bob, who worked for the coal company, had made all the arrangements to purchase a beautiful home for the family. Marna called to say a very important check had been lost. Would we help look for it? The missing cashier's check was several thousand dollars and payable to bearer. They needed the check to take possession of their house.

Cindy and I joined in the search at the large RV they had rented until their home was available. Where had the family been? What had they done? Where was the check last seen? Were there any strangers around? Of course when you are new to town, everyone is a stranger. Marna gave us permission to search anywhere, even her purses. We searched the car, the RV, the suitcases, and anything that seemed like it could hide a scrap of paper. Cindy and I commented how unusual it was to be given permission to rummage through the Kaiser's possessions when they barely knew us.

After several hours of futile searching, we prayed with them and trusted God to restore the lost check. Cindy and I had been home only a few minutes when Bob called. Marna found the check in a forgotten part of her purse. The mystery was solved; the loss restored. The house purchase was completed.

⊠⊠⊠

Oh, I wish all losses could be resolved.

Magnus Otto (M.O.) and Etta Schrieter had been married sixty years. M.O. had recently developed dementia which caused Etta to suffer greatly. She tried to tell the sons that M.O's dementia was serious.

He would say he was going out to take care of the horses but had not owned a horse in over fifty years. He would get lost in his own back yard.

M.O. cashed his social security check and put the money in a secure place. It was so secure that he could not remember where he put it. The elderly couple and their adult children searched the house for days without success. In financial straits due to the lost check, their sons helped them buy groceries for the month.

Etta enjoyed listening to Christian radio broadcasts. She would often sit at the kitchen table with a small transistor radio while she fixed their meals or worked on the church finances. She had been church treasure for twenty five years.

M.O. drew me aside one day and whispered, "Etta is bewitched. She is behaving strangely," he said, "because of that little black box." He was referring to the radio.

He also said, "She is seeing another man, and you better be careful because she will be after you too." I knew it wasn't true.

The sons didn't realize how serious their father's dementia was until Etta was admitted to the hospital due to diverticulitis, a stress induced illness. While recovering her health, Lewis, one of the retired sons came to stay with his dad. Since I had visited often at their home, I knew Lewis also.

"You'll never believe what Dad did last night," Lewis told me.

"I was awakened by Dad's stumbling around the house. I got out of bed, wearing only my underwear, to check on Dad. What's going on, Dad?" I asked him.

M. O. responded with conviction, "We've been robbed. They got my pants." He looked at his son in his underwear and said, "I see they got your pants too!"

Reality may be different than the truth, but to M.O. it was true.

Loss can come because we refuse to face the truth. Linda had run away from home again. Usually fifteen year old girls do not run away. It brought up memories of a girl who had vanished three years before. Her family never heard from her after her disappearance. The rumor was she was in white slavery in Chicago. Her brothers went to Chicago trying to find her but could not. She was only eleven when evil men put their lustful hands around her and took her from the school bus stop. Where was she now? Was she alive? We couldn't help but wonder.

There had been another time Linda had not come home when she was expected. The father of a school friend called and said, "Linda is okay. She just needs some space."

I talked to Linda's mother. She was sure her daughter had not been kidnapped but had gone to a friend's home like she had before. "We thought everything was going okay," she assured me. "The family is happy. We have not been fighting at home."

Unfortunately for Linda and her mother, the guilty party from whom Linda fled was a close friend of the family, and frequent visitor to their home. The shame caused her to flee rather than report to a story of abuse to her parents. She did not return home for several months. She was restored to the family.

Some things need not be reconciled but the past can be healed with new memories. The healing takes place in healthy relationships. Emotional problems are not resolved in running from them. But there is healing of emotions in a safe trusting relationship with Christ.

Jim, the man, who could paralyze catfish by rubbing their bellies, had been a drunkard. He had lost his family, his job, and self-respect. But through the patient love of Jesus, he found forgiveness from his sins and freedom from his addictions. He was restored in all ways but one.

When Jim rode in a car farther than thirty-five miles from home, he got violently sick. He consulted doctors, he prayed, the church prayed for him, but there was no healing from this strange illness. We reasoned there was something attached to his memory from the old life of sin that was present even in his redeemed life. Whenever he got a certain distance from home, he would remember the drunkard he once was, and become ill. Finally he just quit going anywhere beyond thirty-five miles. He was secure in his new life in Christ; it was a small price to pay to not be able to go far from home.

In my humanness, I wished some others would be physically sick when they skipped church or were less than loving. But I am not the King; I am only His knight, carrying out His will to the best of my ability.

⁂

One Sunday evening, a district superintendent from a distant state called. He asked if I would consider coming to pastor in West Virginia. I was happy where I was. The church was growing. I loved the people. I told the DS, "No, and if I ever want to move, I'll call you."

That night I could not sleep. The Lord spoke, "You didn't even ask me."

Throughout the night I struggled and finally told Cindy, "If Dr. Clay, DS of West Virginia, calls back, I'll go."

The next day Dr. Clay called. He said to me, "Young man, I have prayed about this, and you better pray too."

"Dr. Clay," I humbly said. "I have heard from the Lord and I am to come." Dr. Clay invited me to visit the church. "No," I replied, "I am confident God has spoken and I will come without seeing the church."

I let my church know I would be leaving in a month. My brother, Tom, lived five hours to the west, and since we would be moving farther east, he and Karen came to visit us before we left for West Virginia.

Tom and I went golfing early one morning. I had not golfed since college so I borrowed a set of clubs from the neighbor, and we went to a nearby course. The dew was still on the grass.

The first tee overlooked a pond. It was only a short fifty yards over the pond, including the terraced women's tee, between the men's tee and the pond. On my first attempt -- I can't call it a drive -- I hit the top of the ball. It rolled a few feet into the water. I said, "I can do better than that," and retrieved the ball and hit it again with the same results.

By then, my hands were wet from the wet grass and two retrievals from the pond water. The handle of the driver was wet from lying in the grass. I was not a knowledgeable golfer. I should have dried my hands before trying to hit the ball, but I repeated to Tom, "I can do better than that". Again I teed up my wet ball with my wet hands while holding the wet club.

I concentrated. I didn't want to top the ball a third time. I was keyed up. I swung a mighty swing, missed the ball completely, and at the top of the swing, the golf club catapulted from my hands. The club went high into the air, slowly turning around and around, lost momentum, and spiraled into the middle of the pond.

I kept my eyes centered on where the club had disappeared. Tom ran across the bridge to the other side. "Keep your eye on the spot," I shouted.

I had no idea how deep the water would be, but it was a borrowed club, and I had to find it. I stepped into the water and sank into the mud. Still keeping my eyes where I saw the club disappear beneath the water, I slowly stepped toward the middle of the pond, one step at a time. The muck sucked my shoes as I slowly explored the bottom with my feet. With every step I tested the next place where I planned to put my foot. I feared going under the water into a hole, or tripping on a large submerged rock.

The water turned out to be shallow, about four feet deep. It was muddy and impossible to see beneath the surface. I silently prayed, "Oh, Lord, help me." As I reached the center of the pond, the handle of the club flipped up. It had enough air in it to bring it to the surface one time, and I grabbed it with a quick, "Thank you, Lord."

My brother bent over laughing, and when I got to shore, I was so relieved that I could laugh too. We finished our round of golf -- one of us in wet clothes -- then drove home. When we walked into the living room, we both collapsed in laughter on the hard wood floor. We explained to our wives what had happened and laughed again.

The laughter was a gift from God, a release of pent up energy, a letting go of the pastoral pressure of the last two years. It was renewing for the next phase of my ministry.

It was holy laughter. I had some losses. To my sorrow I lost the idealistic trust I had of others with whom I worshipped. I learned that they had feet of clay. Even those with pure hearts at times showed frailties and feared to confront sin.

My gains were so much more. As God's servant I didn't need to be the one who put all things together for the King. With my knight's armor coming off, so did the pressure. I became a shepherd, no longer a knight, and I am content to be one of God's lambs.

LETTERS FROM THE PASTOR

BY
Dr. Blair F. Rorabaugh

Coming soon.

※※※

Praise for *LETTERS FROM THE PASTOR*

Blair:
Your poetic and vivid portrayal of the Roman
Centurion warmed my heart. Thanks for sharing.
Major Brad Lee
Chaplain US Army

※※※

This collection of letters from a pastor to his congregation
deals with many daily incidences. This book is suitable
for devotions and sermon illustrations.

New Floor

Dear Folks,

For some time Cindy has desired a new floor in the kitchen. The old vinyl squares were new when we moved in seven years ago. Over time scratches caught dirt and the floor looked worn. Some of the tiles had cracked. In addition, it was not the color Cindy liked best, but since they were new, she lived with it until they wore out.

Yesterday Cindy and I put down new tile. The floor looks new, clean, fresh, and shiny. Also, it is the right color. In fact, it is so nice and new and clean that I think about how clean it is every time I walk on it. I wish it could stay that way. Unfortunately, I know that in the future I will drag an appliance, leave scuff marks, drop something that stains, and time will tarnish our new, fresh floor.

When I came to Jesus, my heart was dirty. I was unclean. My conscience was guilty. At the age of thirteen, Jesus saved me and gave me a clean heart. He took away my guilty feeling. I wanted to keep my heart clean forever.

Over time, with God's help, and the guidance of Christian parents, Sunday school teachers, pastors, youth leaders, and friends, I learned that sinful actions and attitudes made me feel dirty. I learned that when I sinned, I could confess and change, and my redeemed heart would be like new again. Most importantly, I still want to keep my heart clean.

Your heart can be new again. You can be free from

the bondage of the past, and any scratches will just be a reminder of what God has done for you

I love you.

Pastor.

I John 1:9 If we confess our sins, he is faithful and just and will forgive our sins and cleanse us from all unrighteousness.

Advocate

Dear Folks,

This morning my Dad and I visited the church of my youth in Oil City, Pennsylvania. I remembered something that happened when I was in eighth grade. Of course I was a studious student and always carried home a pile of books. Each morning and evening there was a thirty minutes bus ride to read and do home work assignments. As the bus went from stop to stop, my eyes were down on the book in my lap.

As I got off the bus one afternoon, Mr. Applequist, the bus driver, said to me, "You are suspended from the bus for one week." I asked him why. He said, "You know."

I didn't know what I did to be kicked off the bus. The next day, Mr. Applequist, came to the house and told me I could ride the bus again. No explanation was given.

A few days later my mother asked me if I knew why I was permitted on the bus again. Connie Rice, a high school Senior and our neighbor, had told Mr. Applequist, "It was not Blair that threw the orange."

Mr. Applequist thought it was me because I was looking down and supposed I was the guilty one. Of course I always thought Connie was beautiful. Now I knew she was nice too.

We need an advocate for our transgressions. We also need an advocate when that accuser of the saints, Satan, attacks us to create guilt and confusion. I thank God we have an advocate who defends us even when we are guilty, and stands by us when we are accused falsely.

I love you
Pastor

I John 2: 1b-2 NIV. "We have one who speaks to the Father in our defense– Jesus Christ, the Righteous One. He is the atoning sacrifice for our sins and not only for ours but also for the sins of the whole world."

PS. Cindy edits my writings but this week she is with the grandchildren and I am with my parents. Here are some extra commas. Put them where you think they ought to be.,,,,,,.

Alive or a Floater

Dear Folks,

Mount Hermon, 9,232 ft above sea level, is the highest point in Syria. The southern slopes of Mount Hermon extend to Israel, where the Mount Hermon ski resort is located. A peak in this area rising to 7,336 ft is the highest elevation in Israeli-controlled territory. As a comparison Mount Alyeska, Alaska is 3,939 feet at the ski resort. Because of Mount Hermon's height, it captures a great deal of precipitation in a very dry area of the world. Melt water from the snow-covered mountain's seeps into the rock channels and pores, feeding springs at the base of the mountain.These form streams that merge to become the Jordan River.

Now that information from Wikipedia is just to introduce you to the water flowing from Mount Hermon. It supplies two lakes. One lake is a recreational and commercial area. The shores of the Sea of Galilee welcome swimmers and boaters. There is a thriving fishing industry even today, 2000 years since Peter made a killing with the nets so full they were about to break.

The second lake is dead in that it has no fish or flora. It is called the Dead Sea and is located at the lowest point on earth that is not covered by ocean. There is no scarcity of water. Mount Hermon feeds the Jordan River into it but it has no outflow. The sun evaporates the water and leaves salt. Unlike the Sea of Galilee with its abundant life, the Dead Sea only attracts the curious tourists and those wanting to float on the water for medicinal purposes. There is no grass on the shore, it is desert sand.

Those two lakes are symbolic of our lives. The Holy Spirit flows into us. If we are the giving people God created us to be, we also are channels for the Holy Spirit to flow from us. If we are not channels of God's love, we are belly up floaters. Which are you?

I love you

Pastor

Proverbs 11: 24 One man gives freely, yet gains even more; another withholds unduly, but comes to poverty.

Marathon

Dear Folks,

I was running up Third Street and a man called from a door way, "Are you running Marathon this year?" I told him not that one, but another one. He meant the Fourth of July race up Mount Marathon, and since I lost my place and two years of losing in the lottery – sounds like the preacher has been betting- I decided to keep my money and run other races. But I am running a marathon; in fact, I am running several marathons, but not the twenty six mile or mountain type.

In my marriage, I am running a marathon. Cindy and I are wed for the distance. Forty three years going on sixty and more. When you are in a marathon, there are some things you learn are not as important as going the distance. Thankfully my wife has overlooked or forgiven many of my traits that cause others to give up on me. She still has dreams of training me, "Piano is like pizza." I have heard that clue more times than I know, but when I speak it just doesn't register.

My life with Jesus is a marathon. There are daily surprises, miracles, things I don't understand- why didn't that prayer receive the answer I wanted? I am in the race for the long run. The Christian life is not a sprint, and the Lord has forgiven my sins and cleansed my heart while accepting my inadequate efforts of praise and service.

Does it help you to realize you are running a marathon and not a sprint? There are days of agony, but also days of joy. There are fulfilling days, and days that seem futile, but we will run to the end. We will forgive each other and endure, because we are in a marathon.

I love you,

Pastor

Ecclesiastes 9:9 Live happily with the woman you love through the fleeting days of life, for the wife God gives you is your best reward down here for all your earthly toil. (Living Bible)